Robertson meeting Andreyev on the brokenTorgau roadbridge at 4:00 p.m., April 25, 1945. Ensign George Peck, then Pfc. Frank Huff are sliding down the "V" of the girder behind Robertson. (*Photo by Paul Staub*)

ВСТРЕЧА НА ЭЛЬБЕ

ВОСПОМИНАНИЯ СОВЕТСКИХ И АМЕРИКАНСКИХ УЧАСТНИКОВ ВТОРОЙ МИРОВОЙ ВОЙНЫ

Издательство Агентства печати Новости
Москва, 1988

YANKS
MEET REDS

Recollections of U.S. and Soviet Vets
from the Linkup in World War II

Edited by
MARK SCOTT and
SEMYON KRASILSHCHIK

CAPRA PRESS
SANTA BARBARA
1988

Cover design by Maureen Lauran
Design and typography by Jim Cook

ACKNOWLEDGMENTS

American participation in *Yanks Meet Reds* was made possible through grants from Patrons, who contributed $500 or more to support all the tasks involved in assembling the US sections. In addition to the Patrons, other persons played important roles in assisting the US Editor-in-Chief collect the materials which comprise the American essays in the book. Those individuals include Mr. Robert Swan, Jr., Co-Founder of the Elbe Alliance; Mr. Noel Young, Editor-in-Chief of Capra Press; Mr. Semyon Krasilshchik, USSR Editor-in-Chief of *Meeting at the Elbe;* Mr. LeRoy Wolins, Vice Commander of Vets for Peace; Col. Barney Oldfield; Mr. Oleg Benyukh, editor of *Soviet Life;* Mr. Vladimir Zaryetsky, Information Officer of the Soviet Embassy in Washington, D.C.; Mr. Alexander Malôv of the Soviet War Veterans Committee; Mr. Peter Vincenz, First Secretary, Press and Culture; and Mr. Wolfram Bauer, Cultural Attaché, of the Embassy of the German Democratic Republic in Washington, D.C.; ADN-Zentralbild; and Mayor Horst Strähle and photographer Manfred Bräunlich of Torgau German Democratic Republic.

Segments of JOE POLOWSKY: "We Swore Never to Forget" are taken from Studs Terkel, *The Good War: An Oral History of World War II.* New York: Pantheon Books, 1984. The excerpts are reprinted by permission of Studs Terkel and Pantheon Books, a Division of Random House, Inc.

Excerpts from Andy Rooney's "Trading Day Along the Elbe" are reprinted by permission of *Stars and Stripes.*

Excerpts from Harold Denny's "First Link Made Wednesday by Four Americans on Patrol" are reprinted by permission of the New York Times Company.

Alexei Zhadov's "May this meeting be a guarantee of a stable and lasting peace on our planet!" appears in Zhadov, *Four Years of War.* Moscow:, 1978.

Gleb Baklanov's "The delicious aroma of food expertly prepared mingled with the scent of apple blossoms" is excerpted from Baklanov *The Wind of War.* Moscow: 1977

Ivan Konyev's "The horse I gave Bradley was a handsome and well-trained Don stallion" appears in Konyev, *Notes of a Front Commander.* Moscow: 1981.

The English translation of Yevgeny Yevtushenko's poem "In a Steelworker's Home" is reprinted by permission of The Curtis Publishing Company.

LIBRARY OF CONGRESS CATALOGING-IN-PUBLICATION DATA

Yanks meet Reds: the link-up of U.S. and Soviet troops in Nazi Germany

Mark Chapin Scott, editor

Bibliography: p.   ISBN 0-88496-276-8 (PBK) : $9.95
1. World War, 1939-1945—Personal narratives, American. 2. Soldiers—United States—Bibliography. 3. United States. Army—Bibliography. 4. Soviet Union. Raboche-Krest'ianskaia Krasnaia Armila. 5. Soldiers—Soviet Union—History—20th century. 6. World War, 1939-1945—Campaigns—Elbe River Valley. 7. Elbe River Valley—History. I. Scott, Mark Chapin, 1948-
D811.A2Y355   1988   940.54'81'73—dc19   87-31965 CIP

Published by CAPRA PRESS
Post Office Box 2068, Santa Barbara, California 93120

Dedicated to the Memory of
Joseph Polowsky
1916-1983
Author *Principia* 1935-1936
Participant in the World War II USA-USSR
swearing of the Oath of the Elbe on April 25, 1945
in the area of Torgau, Germany
YANKS MEET REDS:
Recollections of US and Soviet Vets
from the Linkup in World War II

PATRONS
Adventure Bookstore (Lawrence, Kansas)
Mr. Robert Barlett
Dr. James Dray
Mrs. Cyrus Eaton
The Elbe Alliance (Lawrence, Kansas)
Mr. Robert Haag
Mr. Norman Hamm
Mr. Takeru Higuchi
Mr. Glenn Kappelman
Mrs. Andrée McCarty
Professor Charles Michener
Mrs. Mary Michener
Professor Charles Oldfather
Mrs. Hortense Oldfather
Mr. Dillard Powell
Dr. William Robertson
Mr. H.W. Shank
Mrs. Ann Stringer
Mr. Studs Terkel
Mrs. Eleanor Visconsi
Mr. James Whitmore.

CONTENTS

A NOTE FROM THE EDITORS

From America

Two days after American GIs linked up with Soviet soldiers in the heart of Nazi Germany, President Harry S. Truman said in a radio message announcing the historic event, "Nations which can plan and fight together shoulder to shoulder in the face of such obstacles as distance and of language and of communications . . . can live together and work together in the common labor of the organization of the world for peace."

The publication of *Yanks Meet Reds* is evidence that those words spoken more than forty years ago are as true now as they were then. The spirit of the 1945 linkup, the "Spirit of the Elbe," played a crucial role in the success of this book. It united countless individuals representing different countries and ideologies, people from Moscow and Monterey, Torgau and Topeka, Kolki and Kalamazoo, from Unter den Linden to Michigan Avenue. As Allies, they effectively overcame both distance and language to tell us how they first met each other.

Most of our American contributors will say they're not especially extraordinary. They include insurance salesmen, a retired physician, former newspaper reporters, a homemaker, writers, the manager of a men's clothing store, and a wholesale liquor distributor. Despite the passing years, these men and women still vividly recall that day when they first shook hands with "the Russians," when World War II was coming to its long-awaited end, when so many thought permanent peace just around the corner.

These ordinary people, and the many like them, are the true heroes and heroines of this fantastic tale. Some keyboarded their stories for us in modern office buildings on sophisticated word processing machines. Others wrote them in pencil on tablet paper at kitchen tables. One admitted, "I'm not very good at writing, but I'll do my best." Another apologized, "I'm sorry my story's so long. But I just *had* to get it all down." Still others recounted their memories on tape recorders.

And what stories they tell! In them, we repeatedly encounter decent human beings separated by so many different barriers, unable at first to communicate with each other. In spite of the obstacles, however, they finally succeeded in making contact. Are they not like the earthen banks of the River Elbe, divided by bridges which are broken but not severed? And then there is the constant interplay of opposites—East and West, friend and foe, Americans and Soviets, fog and sunlight, horses and jeeps, earth and water, towers overlooking plains, the conqueror and the vanquished. Add human tragedy dramatized by the bizarre union of extremes—boys as soldiers, women in combat. Unintentionally, the stories are often told in the language of ancient symbols. Warriors appear on horseback. Battle-weary legions cross no man's land. There is apocalypse, but also hope resurrected amid the blossoms of spring. Simple words frequently express the profoundest sense of shared humanity.

None of our contributors hesitated to participate in *Yanks Meet Reds*. All of them responded with renewed enthusiasm when they learned that Soviets, East Germans, and West Germans were also taking part in the book. The Europeans, in turn, were encouraged by the enthusiasm of the Americans. I believe that this kind of selfless international cooperation really is proof of the enormous reserves of good will which do exist between millions of human beings throughout the world. As one of our own veterans wrote, "I hope some day all of us will no longer speak of Russians, Americans, Germans, or any other nationalities, but will speak only of *people*. When that time comes, the spirit of brotherhood will truly prevail along the banks of the Elbe, Volga, Mississippi, and every other river on this our earth."

MARK SCOTT, U.S. EDITOR-IN-CHIEF

From the Soviet Union

From the pages of this book, young faces look out at us, faces of soldiers of 1945—year of the Great Victory over Hitler fascism, the cruelest enemy of all peace-loving peoples. On April 25th, the Soviet and American armies united in a single thrust near the town of Torgau on the Elbe—in the very heart of Germany. This historic event was the culmination of that wartime cooperation between the governments of the anti-Hitler coalition that had evolved so successfully throughout the war. It was the culmination of their unity and common resolve to win final victory over the forces of hatred, destruction, and evil.

Underscoring the historic significance of the meeting of the allied armies, the heads of state of the anti-Hitler coalition—the USSR, USA, and Great Britain—delivered special addresses. In Moscow, 324 artillery pieces fired in a twenty-four-salvo salute.

Meanwhile, emotional, joyous meetings between soldiers of the two armies were still going on at the Elbe. Friendly handshakes, fraternal embraces—this was indeed the stellar hour in the lives of hundreds and thousands of soldiers of the allied armies. People separated by ideologies and language were overwhelmed by feelings of brotherhood and unity in their quest for peace.

Even now, several decades later, Soviet and American veterans cannot forget the atmosphere of sincerity of that time. The reminiscences of those who participated in the meetings at the Elbe (some of them, unfortunately, no longer with us) form the basis of this book. A number of sections have been written expressly for this publication. Others were written many years ago. Among the contributors are generals and privates, professional writers and people who have taken up the pen for the first time. Naturally, their reminiscences in some ways repeat each other, but somehow differ. Yet the authors have one thing in common—they survived the gunfire of war and in all candor have recounted the memories they have since carried with them. Years can erase the insignificant details. But that which was most important shall forever remain— the Oath taken in April 1945, the Oath pledging to do everything possible to strengthen the friendship between the peoples of the USSR and USA, not to allow another war ever to occur.

For the soldiers of the US First Army, it was a path of thorns from Normandy to the Elbe. But longer and more bloody yet was that road traveled by units of the Red Army from Stalingrad to the Elbe. Having met in April of 1945 as comrades in arms, soldiers of the two armies have remained loyal friends even in peacetime. Their life's goal has been what humanity values above all else—peace on earth.

General Dwight Eisenhower wrote in his book *Crusade in Europe* that the war had essentially brought together the peoples of our countries, and that this was something to cherish and never forget . . . Unfortunately, for reasons both objective and subjective, Soviet-American relations after the Second World War have often been clouded, strained. But even in the most difficult periods of the "cold war" Soviet and American veterans of the Elbe linkup have remained faithful to their friendship and to the Oath they first took in 1945 and repeated at the same place in 1985—"In memory of those who perished on the battlefields, and of those who are no more, and on behalf of their descendants, let us spare no effort in averting war!"

SEMYON KRASILSHCHIK, USSR EDITOR-IN-CHIEF

1. From Normandy

to the Elbe

Edited by Mark Scott

INTRODUCTION

"This is It, kid, this is The Day, all the way from Newburyport to Vladivostok." So boomed the jubilant voice of an American GI over CBS Radio on the night of May 8, 1945. It was The Day—Victory Day in Europe. The Thousand-Year Reich smashed. Hitler dead. Germany in ruins. The Little Guy had triumphed over the Supermen.

But the first Victory Day celebrations took place not in Washington, Moscow, London, or Paris. They were hosted by neither presidents, prime ministers, nor generals. They broke out on their own in late April in small, isolated communities along Germany's Elbe River. The celebrants—quite ordinary people—were American GIs and soldiers of the Red Army.

They were friends then. They are friends now. This is their story. They had advanced from opposite ends of the globe to link up in the heart of Nazi Germany. Their coming together in the spring of 1945 cut the Third Reich in half, thereby effectively ending the Second World War in Europe. This they knew, and this they celebrated on Their Day more than a week before the rest of the world rejoiced.

Peace at last. "No one is firing from the west," thought Alexander Olshansky on that day at Strehla, "and no one is firing from the east—no one." Bill Robertson remembered thinking when he met Soviet troops at Torgau, "All of us would live another hour, another day."

And what remarkable days they were when Yanks met Reds! A time of joyful exhilaration signifying an end to the most destructive war in history. From the west, Allied armies had crossed the English channel in a mighty armada and shed their blood on the beaches of Normandy in the face of an armored Nazi phalanx. By land and by air, Anglo-American forces knifed their way into the fascist homeland. From the east, the Red Army—in Churchill's words—"tore the guts out of the German military machine." Soviet fighting men joined by Soviet fighting women battled heroically from a besieged Moscow, a starved Leningrad, from the snowy graveyard of Stalingrad. Some, such as Sgt. Alexander Olshansky, walked the entire distance until they met their American comrades in arms.

On April 25, 1945, Olshansky was with the first Soviet soldiers to link up with an American patrol. It was led by Lt. Buck Kotzebue, and included his German interpreter, Pvt. Joe Polowsky. The two sides met on the east bank of the Elbe amid the charred bodies of German refugees. Deeply moved by the scene of these civilian dead, the American and Soviet soldiers took an Oath of the Elbe pledging to do all they could to prevent a future world war. That same day, another important linkup occurred far away in San Francisco—the United Nations was born. Both the Meeting at the Elbe and the birth of the UN caused millions of people everywhere to hope for a lasting peace. Few of those at the Elbe or in San Francisco envisioned that the ensuing peace would be as troubled as it has been. And no one realized that the meetings along the Elbe would be the last time the armies of the United States and Soviet Union would meet strictly as friends.

Yet beyond the historical significance of the linkups, those meetings were of far more compelling interest from a human standpoint. It was the Little Guy's day, when small things suddenly became large. Even villages hard to locate on the best maps of Germany became of international importance; places such as Clanzschwitz, Leckwitz, and Zausswitz. Nor will you find in most history books the names of the Americans and Soviets who joined hands at the Elbe. Just look for Joe Polowsky, Grigory Goloborodko, Bill Shank, Nikolai Andréyev, Cecil Ellzey, the pilot Titov, Ann Stringer, Alexander Silvashko, George Peck, Ben Casmere and Poochie.

On "Elbe Day," human beings who were farthest from the seats of power met in an ecstatic outpouring of pure emotion. The heart ruled the head as American soldiers in search of "the Russians" almost arrogantly disobeyed orders not to exceed a five-mile patrol limit. It was frequently a day without anger, without hatred—a day of love. "I never kissed so many men in my life," Ben Casmere recalled. Bill Robertson characterized the atmosphere of his meeting with Soviet troops as a "one-world feeling." Art Long remembered, "We were on the same side. Everybody was a friend."

It was a day when military protocol became one big party. "We drank and there were accordions and balalaikas and music and dancing," Joe Polowsky recalled. "The Russians played American songs. Some of the other guys could play the guitar. And there were some from slave-labor camps. Russian girls dancing. A strange sight. I was so captivated by the event that it took possession of me for the rest of my life." Reporting on the Torgau festivities of April 26, war correspondent Andy Rooney wrote, "The Russian soldiers are the most carefree bunch of screwballs that ever came together in an army. They could best be described as exactly like Americans, only twice as much. . . ." When asked how they were getting along with the GIs, the Soviet soldiers at the Elbe often replied, "The Americans are down-to-earth and enjoy a good drink."

Yes, that was The Day, kid, when opposites were for the moment reconciled. In the Spirit of the Elbe—the spirit of unsullied brotherhood—East met West, Communist met Capitalist, Believer met Non-Believer, man met woman. Soviet General Vladimir Rusakov feted Texan reporter Ann Stringer, who in almost fairy-tale fashion had "descended from the sky." Cleveland veteran Albert Hornyak vividly related, "I danced with a Russian girl with a machine gun over her shoulder."

What does this mean to younger generations now, long after U.S. and Soviet troops met in fascist Germany? In a television program marking the fortieth anniversary of the event, British commentator Jonathan Dimbleby observed, "Once, what happened here set the world rejoicing. Now, it's like a far-off tale of make-believe. But here at the Elbe, it remains a difficult story to ignore."

Chicago taxi driver Joe Polowsky could not ignore it. For years after the war, he stood every April 25—often alone—on the Michigan Avenue bridge urging everyone he met to join with him in renewing the Oath of the Elbe. "When I stand there," he said, "I pass out a statement: 'Halt the spread of nuclear weapons.' If a passerby asks who I am, I tell him about the Meeting at the Elbe." In the Spirit of the Elbe, Joe unsuccessfully lobbied the United Nations to have April 25 officially recognized as "Elbe Day," an international day of peace. He died of cancer in 1983, and was buried according to his wishes in Torgau.

Although separated now by time, geography, language, and ideology, the men and women who met more than forty years ago in a devastated Germany still believe that peace and reconciliation are possible for humanity, especially today. "We are convinced," Maj. Gen. Alexander Olshansky said in 1985, "that the Spirit of the Elbe lives. The spirit of our military service as allies lives. We are convinced that we can live in peace when it is essential to do so." Lt. Col. Buck Kotzebue added:

"I think there is definitely something soldiers have in common. Namely, the realization of what war is, and the fact that if it were left up to them, there wouldn't be any wars.

That was The Day, kid, when impossible dreams came true, when peace was stronger than war, life stronger than death, love stronger than hate. The day of the Little Guy—a day for everyone. That's what this book is really about. The impossible might not be so impossible after all.

—MARK SCOTT,
U.S. Editor-in-Chief

Polowsky (*standing*) with Soviet and U.S. soldiers at Kreinitz, April 25, 1945.

1. Joe Polowsky

"We swore never to forget."

I was a rifleman, private, Company G, 273rd Infantry, Third Platoon, Sixty-ninth Division, First Army. We had seen plenty of action. We were in a quiet area along the Mulde River, a tributary of the Elbe. A town called Trebsen, twenty miles west of the Elbe.

April 24, 1945. I was called into Company headquarters. They were checking on documents of Germans, suspects, former Nazis, and those who wanted to be officials. I was the only man in the Company who had a good working knowledge of German.

A phone call comes in from Battalion headquarters. They want a patrol to be formed immediately—seven jeeps, twenty-eight men— to go about five miles in front of the lines to see if they could get some signs of the Russians. They were supposed to be anywhere from twenty to thirty miles in front of us. Actually, we weren't even supposed to meet the Russians. If we did meet them, we were going to take the consequences in case anything was fouled up. At Eisenhower's headquarters, they were making detailed plans to meet the Russians. We were just on patrol. We were told that after five miles, we were going at our own risk. If anything went awry, instead of being heroes we might wind up being court-martialed.

They were afraid if the two armies met at full speed, there would be casualties. Two armies, even friendly armies, going hellbent toward each other, there would be some guys who would be hurt. So Eisenhower and Zhukov decided that the two armies would stop about twenty-five miles short of each other. That's why we stopped at the Mulde and they at the Elbe.

The best platoon leader in our Company—by general consensus— was Lt. Kotzebue. He was quiet, young—about twenty-five years old. I was twenty-six. He quickly assembled the jeeps and the men. He took a map of the area. I was in the lead jeep with him because I spoke German. We were warned before we left that platoons from other companies had been badly shot up by the Germans in this region.

We were seventy miles south from Berlin where the Battle of Berlin was being waged. Every available German soldier was called up to defend Berlin. We ran into many deserters, however. A continual stream, some of them actually dressed in women's clothing. The great mass was the German civilian refugees fleeing west. They were continually blocking the road. Mostly women, children, and old men.

To show you how slowly we proceeded, we had just managed to get about seven miles, and we'd started about noon. We holed up in a little town called Kühren. Kotzebue pored over the maps all evening. We interrogated anybody who had any idea where the Russians might be.

When we holed up for the night, we'd gone only a third of the way. As dawn broke, Kotzebue made a decision: we're going ahead. There was a tremendous cheer. We all hopped in the jeeps and proceeded. We didn't know what faced us. At noon, we also saw long streams of liberated civilians from concentration camps, slave laborers, and Allied soldiers who were freed.

Would you believe it? There was a tremendous burst of lilacs as we approached the Elbe River. This exaltation of being alive, after all those days trapped in a trench war. There were even jokes that we were approaching the River Jordan, crossing into Canaan. Of course, we were saddened to learn that President Roosevelt had died two weeks earlier. We also knew that the United Nations was being born in San Francisco on the very same day, the 25th of April. Can you imagine? The very day we linked up with the Russians at the Elbe River.

It was a tremendous feeling to see the Elbe. This was about 11:30 in the morning.[1] The Elbe is a swift-running river, about 175 yards wide. Kotzebue shot up two green flares. After about ten minutes—with shouts and the wind blowing towards the east—our voices were able to carry across the river. The Russians waved and gave us the signal to approach their lines. The problem was getting across the river. The Germans in retreat, the Allied forces dropping bombs along the bridges, the Russian artillery blowing up the bridges—between the three, there was no bridge to cross.

We were at Strehla, about sixteen miles south of Torgau. At the far side of the Elbe—the Russian side—there was the remains of a steel bridge which jutted out maybe fifty yards into the river. On our side, there was a heavy chain attached to a barge and two sailboats. With a hand grenade, Kotzebue exploded the chain. Six of us piled into the sailboat.[2] There were makeshift paddles. With tremendous effort, we managed to guide the boat into the girders protruding from the opposite side. As we climbed up, three Russian soldiers were approaching the bank. Why only three? On the road ahead, we saw many Russian soldiers.

Fifty yards on each side of us was literally covered with bodies—of women, old men, children. I still remember seeing a little girl clutching a doll in one hand—it was right there. She couldn't have been more than five or six years old. And her mother's hand in the other. They were all piled up like cordwood at the bank.

How had it happened? Who knows? That bridge had been blown up at least three days. Part of it was German fire, maybe Allied planes bombing the bridgehead. Probably the Russian artillery from a distance of several miles. It was a depressed area—impossible to see. It was an accident. There were so many in the war.

Actually, it was difficult for the Russians to get through to us because of the bodies. Here we are, tremendously exhilarated, yet there's a sea of dead. Kotzebue, a very religious man, was much moved. He couldn't talk Russian. The Russians couldn't talk English. He said, "Joe, let's make a resolution with these Russians here and also the ones on the bank: this would be an important day in the lives of the two countries and the symbolism of all the civilian dead. Talk to them in German." As I was translating to Kotzebue in English, one of the Russians who knew German was translating to the other Russians. At this historic moment of the meeting of nations, all of the soldiers present—ordinary soldiers, Americans and Russians—solemnly swore that they would do everything in their power to prevent such things from ever happening in the world again. We pledged that the nations of the world would and must live at peace. This was our Oath of the Elbe.

It was a very informal, but solemn moment. There were tears in the eyes of most of us. Perhaps a sense of foreboding that things might not be as perfect in the future as we anticipated. We embraced. We swore never to forget.

When we got to the top of the embankment, there stood Lt. Col. Gordeyev. He greeted us, and again we took the oath. Kotzebue's main mission was to contact the Americans immediately. Our radios were in the jeeps on the other side of the Elbe. So Gordeyev said go and come back. We'd been drinking and embracing and toasting. The Russians had brought some vodka and some German wine and beer. We were real drunk, but not because of the liquor. Gordeyev said, "It's important you tell the others. After you've done that, pile into your jeeps, cross onto a ferry, and we'll continue our celebration." He sent a couple of Russians to accompany us.

As soon as we got across, Kotzebue gets in touch with headquarters. He gave them readings where we were at Strehla. But there was radio interference. As often happens, radio communications in combat rarely work perfectly. An hour passed. We're getting impatient. He wants to make firm contact with the American forces to either bring the Russians back to the American lines or Americans to come up.

After we made the communications, we piled into the jeeps with the two Russian guys.[3] We went about three, four miles north into this hand ferry. We all crossed again into the Russian lines. As we crossed the bank, Kotzebue tossed me the map. He said, "You've done a good job. Here's a little present for you." I kept it as a souvenir. I was actually offered a very considerable sum of money for it. Of course, I wouldn't dream of giving it up. It's not for sale.

As we learned later, there were mixed feelings on the part of the American headquarters. We weren't supposed to meet the Russians. They were, of course, secretly glad that we met them without casualties. They really dispatched a helicopter to Strehla, but there were only seven jeeps.[4] Something had been fouled up. Meanwhile, there are tremendous celebrations in the Russian lines.

We drank and there were accordions and balalaikas and music and dancing. They played American songs. Some of the other guys could play the guitar. And there were some from slave-labor camps. Russian girls dancing. It was a strange sight. I was so captivated by the event that it took possession of me for the rest of my life. It has colored my life, in spite of difficulties I've run into—general indifference.

There was another patrol of Lt. Robertson. He and three others in a jeep made the main contact with the Russians. He arrived at the Soviet lines at 4:30 in the afternoon, four hours after we met the Russians. A great celebration occurred. This was the only patrol mentioned in the communiqué of Truman, Churchill, and Stalin. Robertson was able to get four Russians into his jeep and go back to the American lines. He raced back to Trebsen. Nearly four hundred American and Allied correspondents were champing at the bit. They knew something was up and were just waiting to break the news the whole world had been waiting for since Stalingrad. Since Normandy. It was a moving and a wonderful thing . . . But there was this special thing of the Oath of the Elbe. It would have been better.

They were also angry when Robertson got back. But they got over it fast. There'd been a news blackout, in effect, because they wanted to wait until Truman, Churchill, and Stalin made the announcement. It was better the way it happened. When ordinary soldiers meet, as we met and Robertson met, it's more informal. That's the way armies should meet.

I always felt that American-Russian relations were plagued by bad luck from the beginning. If we had gotten publicity with the Oath of the Elbe, there would have been a certain depth in the feelings. Just think of the millions who died on the Russian side and the tremendous effort on the American side, amidst all those dead women and children and that little girl clutching the doll in her hand.

When I stand on the Michigan Avenue bridge every April 25, I pass out a statement: "Halt the spread of nuclear weapons." If a passerby asks who I am, I tell him about the Meeting at the Elbe. I'll be at the bridge next April 25, God willing.

There is a memorial in Torgau. It must be a good two stories high. It shows Americans and Russians shaking hands. It has the American flag on one side and the Russian flag on the other. It's on a beautiful stretch of green, right as the Elbe River flows. I'm getting to be an old man. I will be buried at Torgau.

JOSEPH POLOWSKY abandoned botany studies at the University of Chicago in 1947 to lead what was often a penniless, one-man crusade against the Cold War. A Taft Republican, Polowsky founded the tiny American Veterans of the Elbe River Linkup and wrote thousands of letters to journalists and public officials urging them to remember the Oath of the Elbe. He lobbied the United Nations tirelessly, yet unsuccessfully to have April 25 officially declared "Elbe Day"—a day of international peace.

Polowsky became known to millions of people in the United States and Soviet Union as the Chicago taxi driver who stood each April 25 on the Michigan Avenue bridge to renew his Oath of the Elbe and encourage others to join with him in pledging to do all they could to prevent another world war. He died of cancer on October 18, 1983, and was buried in Torgau the following month. "His gravesite," his close friend LeRoy Wolins writes, "has become a world peace shrine."

1. The Kotzebue Patrol met the lone Soviet horseman—Aitkalia Alibekov—in Leckwitz at approximately 11:30 A.M. The patrol reached the Elbe at about noon.
2. Seven men boarded the sailboat. They were Kotzebue, Polowsky, Ruff, Wheeler, Hamlin, Kowalski, and the newly-liberated Polish POW.
3. Four Soviet officers re-crossed the Elbe with the Americans. The group of four included a lieutenant colonel of infantry, a major of engineers, an artillery captain, and a newsreel photographer.
4. Gen. Reinhardt, commander of the U.S. Sixty-ninth Division, dispatched liaison planes—not a helicopter—to Groba, the town mistakenly reported to have been the linkup site.

2. BUCK KOTZEBUE

(Soviet War Veterans Committee.)

"We waded knee-deep through the bodies of German refugees."

At approximately 4:00 P.M. on April 24, I received a phone call from Capt. George Caple, commanding officer of G Company. He instructed me to pick up seven jeeps and immediately take a twenty-seven man patrol east of the Mulde River.

I reported with my patrol to Battalion headquarters at Trebsen, where Maj. Fred Craig—the executive officer—told me that my mission was "to contact the Russians." Because American troops at the Mulde had been ordered to go no farther than five miles east of the river, I was assigned to patrol as far as the town of Kühren in search of Russian units. If we made contact, I was to arrange a meeting as soon as possible between their CO, and Col. Charles Adams, commander of the 273rd Infantry.

Leaving Trebsen at about 4:30 P.M., we drove northeast to Kühren. At Burkartshain, we disarmed seventy-five demoralized German soldiers and sent them back to Trebsen. We also found a hospital which housed American, British, Polish, French, and other Allied POWs. They were too seriously wounded to be evacuated to the rear, but their enthusiasm for us was great when they saw

23

our uniforms. Some cheered, others cried. All smiled—they were finally free.

Our patrol left Burkartshain at 5:30 P.M. for Kühren. We entered the town without firing a shot, despite the fact that Kühren was full of German soldiers. None offered any resistance. We rounded up about 350 of them, as well as a large number of wounded soldiers scattered in houses throughout the village.

I radioed Regiment what we had found. Shortly thereafter, I received instructions from Headquarters to patrol a five-mile radius of Kühren in search of Russians or more German soldiers. To accomplish this new mission, I left most of the patrol in the town with the POWs, and took a two-jeep patrol in the direction of Deutsch-Luppa. On the way, we came upon a farmhouse occupied by some fifteen British POWs, who told us that there was no German resistance between the American and Russian lines. The Brits had heard that the Russians might be at Oschatz or at the town of Strehla, located on the west bank of the Elbe River.

When we reached Deutsch-Luppa, a German civilian rode up on a motorcycle. Trying to ingratiate himself with us, he reported that a German officer was at that moment escaping in a car to the northeast. We swung our jeeps to the north, saw the vehicle speeding away, and gave chase. The jeeps followed in a wild ride, with machine guns firing. The German raced through a roadblock at a railroad crossing. Not wanting to risk being ambushed, I ordered the patrol to slow down. This gave the German time to escape, and ultimately prevented us from returning to Trebsen that night.

Driving at full speed, we arrived back in Kühren at 9:00 P.M. Regiment had radioed me two messages to return to Trebsen before nightfall. But because we had received the messages after dark, I decided to spend the night in Kühren. The patrol stayed in three houses still occupied by their owners.

The next morning—April 25—our German "hosts" prepared us a breakfast of fresh eggs and bacon. At nine o'clock, I took five jeeps east, leaving two jeeps behind to maintain radio contact with Regiment.

Leaving Kühren that cold April morning, I had no orders to go farther east. Instead, I was broadly interpreting my original instructions "to contact the Russians." Because there appeared to be no resistance between the Mulde and the Elbe, and since rumors had it that the Russians were so close, I thought that my patrol might as well go ahead and try to make contact. Besides, I had a special personal interest in the Russian people. One of my ancestors, the playwrite August von Kotzebue, had been a court favorite of Russian Empress Catherine the Great. Another Russian relative, the navigator Otto von Kotzebue, had discovered Kotzebue Sound off the northwest coast of Alaska.

The patrol drove north to Dahlen, where we captured thirty-one Germans, several of whom said they knew the short cut to Strehla. I ordered these "guides" to sit on the hoods of our jeeps, and we took off for Strehla. We passed through Lampertswalde, then across a series of country roads, and arrived in the tiny village of Leckwitz. Driving up the main street, I saw a lone horseman a few hundred yards away. He disappeared into a courtyard.

He looked strangely out of place. Was this it?

The jeeps spun around to the entrance of the courtyard. There— amid a ragged crowd of displaced persons—sat a Russian soldier on a horse. The time was 11:30 A.M.[2]

This was the first reported contact between the armies of the United States and Soviet Union.

The soldier was a cavalryman. He was quiet, reserved, unenthusiastic. When I asked him where his commandant was, we waved his arm toward the east. The Russian told me that his CP was farther to the southeast. He said a newly-freed Polish POW there with him could lead us faster to the CP[3] than he could. The Pole happily accepted the assignment.

With the Pole on the hood of the lead jeep, we drove at full speed to the road just north of Strehla which goes to the Elbe. Traveling down this road for several hundred yards, we spotted the river, then strained our eyes looking across it. I could see the remnants of a pontoon bridge and the wreckage of a column of vehicles on a road paralleling the east bank. People were walking around the debris.

I ordered the patrol to stop. Everyone piled out of the jeeps. I looked through my field glasses, and saw men in brown shirts. I knew they were Russians, because someone had once told me that Russians wore their medals into battle. Medals on the brown shirts were reflecting sunlight. Yes, these were Russians. The time was 12:05 P.M.

Turning to Pfc. Ed Ruff, I told him to fire two green flares—the recognition signal which the American and Russian armies had previously agreed upon. The Americans were to fire green flares, the Russians red. Ruff's flares soared over the Elbe from the launcher attached to the end of his carbine.

The Russians did not respond with red flares. Instead, all of them began walking from the road down to the river bank. I told Ruff to fire another green flare, which he did. The Pole began wildly shouting "*Amerikanski!*" at the top of his voice. The Russians yelled at us to cross the river.

The pontoon bridge had been blown on the west bank of the Elbe; half of it still jutted out onto the river from the east bank. The only way to cross was by boat. Not far from where we stood, two barges and two sailboats had been chained to the shore. Because we couldn't unfasten them by hand, I balanced a grenade on the knot of chains, pulled the pin, and took cover. The explosion cut the chains and freed the sailboats.

Seven of us got into one of the boats. In addition to myself and Pfc. Ruff, the group included Pfc. Jack Wheeler, a machine gunner; Pvt. Larry Hamlin, a rifleman; medic Steve Kowalski, brought along as a Russian interpreter; my German interpreter, Pfc. Joe Polowsky; and the Pole.

We shoved the sailboat from the shore upstream of the bridge. The current moved us swiftly down the river. Fighting the current with makeshift paddles, we finally nosed into the gap between the bridge's two end floats. A Russian soldier there on the bridge leaned out and threw us a line. I later learned he was Sgt. Alexander Olshansky.

After fastening the boat to the pontoon, we got out and met Sgt. Olshansky; his company commander, Maj. Grigory Goloborodko; and a captain who was a news photographer. To reach the Russian soldiers coming down to the bridge to greet us, we literally waded knee-deep through the bodies of German refugees who had been killed by accident when either the bridge exploded, the nearby vehicles were bombed, or misdirected artillery fire struck the river bank.

Our initial meeting with the Russians was very formal. We exchanged salutes and shook hands. I explained to Maj. Goloborodko through Kowalski that we were an American patrol, that we had come from Trebsen to make contact with the Russian army, and that I had been instructed to arrange a meeting between the

American and Russian commanders as soon as possible. The time was 12:30 P.M.

Maj. Goloborodko reported that his regimental commander, Lt. Col. Alexander Gordeyev, had already been notified of our arrival. He was on his way. Within moments, we all became more at ease, smiling and exchanging compliments. While we waited for the regimental commander, the Russian photographer had us pose for a few pictures.

Col. Gordeyev arrived. As he walked up to me, I saluted and reported that I was the leader of an American patrol which had come to make contact with his army. Gordeyev returned my salute and shook hands. We exchanged speeches on how proud we were to be there, how historic this moment was for both our countries.

I then repeated the information to Gordeyev that I had told Maj. Goloborodko. The Colonel said that his Army's mission was to close a pincers movement around Dresden. His regiment had been at the Elbe for several days. They had been ordered by higher authority not to cross the river. Gordeyev had, he said, been waiting for the Americans to make contact. He knew nothing of our orders not to exceed the five-mile limit of the Mulde.

In the village of Lorenzkirch, I met the Russian adjutant, who congratulated me on the linkup. He instructed me to re-cross the river with our Russian officers. They would guide us three miles north to meet the General. At 1:05 P.M., we boarded the same sailboat and crossed the Elbe.

On the west bank, all of us—including the four Russians—got into the five jeeps and headed north to the ferry-crossing opposite the town of Kreinitz. Before boarding the ferry, I ordered platoon sergeant Fred Johnston back to Kühren to answer any questions from Regiment concerning the linkup. I sent the following radio message: "Mission accomplished. Making arrangements for meeting between CO's. Present location (8717). No casualties."[4]

The message was sent at 1:30 P.M. It was received at 3:15. By mistaking Strehla for Groba on my map, I had radioed incorrect coordinates to Regiment.

We drove one of the jeeps onto the wooden platform of the ferry, then pulled it across the Elbe by ropes stretching from one shore to the other. A crowd of Russians gathered on the east bank. Photographers were taking motion pictures of us as we approached. We ferried three jeeps to the Russian side of the river, then drove to Mühlberg—headquarters of the 175th Regiment. The CP was in a large farmhouse. A banquet table had already been set. Everyone was in the festive "Spirit of the Elbe," a spirit of comradeship, mutual sacrifice, happiness, and relief that the war would soon be at an end. Maj. Gen. Vladimir Rusakov came in shortly. We toasted the late President Roosevelt, President Truman, Prime Minister Churchill, Marshal Stalin, and "everlasting friendship" between us all.

After much celebrating, I had my patrol get into the three jeeps for the first leg of our return to Trebsen. When we reached the ferry, we saw more jeeps on the west bank. I thought that my radio jeep had returned with other vehicles. But when I entered the house on the east bank which was serving as the Russian battalion CP, I met Maj. Craig, Capt. Morey, Lt. Howard, and Capt. Fox. Because Col. Adams radioed us to "hold in abeyance until further orders all arrangements for meeting," we remained at our location. Unknown to us, a second linkup had already taken place to our north—at Torgau.

ALBERT L. ("BUCK") KOTZEBUE pursued a military career after the war, serving in both Korea and Vietnam. He retired from the Army in 1967 with the rank of Lt. Col. Kotzebue died in Monterey, California, on March 19, 1987.

1. CO is the abbreviation for Commanding Officer.
2. The lone horseman was a soldier from Soviet Central Asia—Aitkalia Alibekov of Kazakhstan.
3. CP is the abbreviation for Command Post.
4. The message Kotzebue wanted to send was "We cut the bastards in half." However, his radio operator, Staff Sergeant William E. Weisel of Norwood, Ohio, insisted on standard Army terminology.

3. BILL SHANK

"The Russians came running over to the jeep, hugging and kissing us and chattering at the top of their voices."

In april 1945, I was a First Lt., Combat Liaison Officer with the 104th Mechanized Cavalry Reconnaissance Troop of the 104th (Timberwolf) Infantry Division. By order of VII Corps, the Division stopped on the west bank of the Mulde River, with HQ[1] at the town of Delitzsch. Division thought the Russians were east of the Elbe, but did not know exactly where. Lt. Gen. Collins, the Corps commander, wanted to determine if there were any patrols operating between the Elbe and the Mulde. He asked our Division commander, Maj. Gen. Terry de la Mesa Allen, if anyone could find out. Gen. Allen told him he had just the man who could do it.

Right after lunch on April 23, my CO Capt. Laundon and I received a call from Maj. Fosnot, Assistant G-2.[2] A decision was subsequently made to send three men out on a special mission. Cpl. Jack Solowitz of the Medics was one; he spoke German. A freed Russian POW was the second. And I became the third. Our orders were to penetrate as far east as Torgau on the Elbe in search of the Russians.

The three of us proceeded that night to an outpost at Wellaune, about three miles northeast of HQ and three miles west of the Mulde. There we left two armored cars whose radios were tuned to different frequencies in the hope that if we met the Russians we might make radio contact with HQ. With riflemen at our back for protection, we boarded an assault boat and got out on the east bank of the Mulde. The time was 10:30 P.M.

To our south, Divarty (Division artillery) was plastering a town with white phosphorous shells. I had selected a route that took us northeast, then due east to Torgau. Except for the first three miles, our route went almost entirely through forest, avoiding towns and parallel roads.

A half-moon shone occasionally. We traveled by stars and compass. By 1:30 in the morning, we had encountered nothing but a dog and a horse and wagon. We had skirted three communities and crossed two lateral roads. The first one was lined with wires singing with business. Crossing the second, we entered a forest which turned out to be a swamp. So as not to get off course, we waded straight on. Although the distance seemed to be rising, the water was actually getting deeper—we were wading up to our waists. But the three of us had come too far to go back.

Almost at the end of our endurance, we crossed a creek, another lateral road, then entered a field. For a short time, woods alternated with fields. As we left some trees, the moon exposed a very large field which lay on our route. It turned out to be another swamp, so we skirted it to woods to the south. About a half mile into this forest, a voice in German ordered us to halt.

We could have avoided them. But then we would have had the problem of trying to cross any communication net they put up. And we would never know what we had run into. Besides, there was an outside chance they were Russians. Anyway, I hadn't come entirely unprepared. We responded with *freunden* and advanced to a small clearing where three *Wehrmachten* trained rifles on us. More appeared. I wore the flap of my holster pinned back—for months, I had been practicing my draw everywhere I went. The hammer of my .45 was cocked. For an instant, I thought that if things got depressing, I might try my luck. And I remember wondering how it would affect my mother if I were to throw my life away in the last days of the war. Besides, this wasn't what we had come for.

I asked to see the commandant. A man in civies appeared. He said he was a technician, and seemed to have authority. I needed to come up with a good story—fast. I told them, through Cpl. Solowitz, that it was only a matter of hours until the Russian and American forces would meet. Resistance was, I said, senseless and useless. I stressed that we had come with the express purpose of preventing unnecessary loss of life, that they should proceed to the troops following us and surrender. We would continue on and advise other German units to do likewise.

After a lot of palaver, our captors began to agree to my proposition—all except their ramrod sergeant. He insisted that it was a matter for the Lieutenant. I said, "Well, get him!" The Lieutenant was away somewhere, so they sent someone for him. While one of them was looking for the Lieutenant, things got pretty cozy. The sergeant assured us that the Lieutenant would see it our way.

The Lieutenant couldn't be found. So I told the Sergeant it was up to him. But the stubborn goat wouldn't take the responsibility. He said he would have to take it up with Headquarters. This was getting a little hairy, but HQ was in the right direction, and we were getting information. We picked up a forest road and started out in the bright moonlight with eight or ten German soldiers following, chattering like high school kids coming back from a football game.

Near daylight of the 24th, we arrived at an SS *Totenkopf* ("Death Head") HQ. I was seated at a desk. A Panzer lieutenant came over and started berating me. I tried to tell him my mission-of-mercy story, but this was obviously no place for it. Another lieutenant came over and shook his fist in my face. He told me what he thought of us for starting the bombing of cities. I told him we didn't start it, but would like to stop it and all further loss of life and property. He became more and more belligerent, and I began thinking about my mother again. I was in over my head this time, up against forces I had no possibility of influencing. However, things finally quieted down after my interrogators had vented their spleen. They began to talk more sympathetically.

It was six o'clock on the morning of April 24. I finally said it was obvious we had no common ground on which to continue the discussion. I said I would return to my command and convey my impressions. They replied that I most certainly would not. I then asked permission to carry my plan to the next higher HQ. Amazingly, they agreed. They put us in the back seat of a Mercedes-Benz with the two lieutenants in the front. A double motorcycle escort traveled in front of and behind the car.

The Germans drove us back and forth over the very territory we had come to reconnoiter. We saw two colonels in succession, told them our story, and were each time referred to the next higher command. It became a joke. We drove twice through Torgau. On the morning of the 24th, the bridge over the Elbe was still intact and guarded. The streets were barricaded. The town was under artillery fire; our guides told us the Russians were twelve kilometers east of the river. We were freezing from swamp water.

On our second trip through Torgau, the car stopped in front of a *schloss* near the bridge. An impressive-looking individual took us in tow and put us in a nice warm room with fifteen American GIs lying on mattresses; I've always wondered whatever became of them. This looked like the end of the road. I started yelling and beating on the door.

A guard came and wanted to know what was the matter. I demanded to see the commandant. I told him that we had come on a matter of diplomatic service, that it was *outrageous* that we should be treated like this. I told him a serious mistake had been made, and insisted on seeing the commandant. Cpl. Solowitz must have done a good job of getting this across, because the guard said we would have to see the General. They loaded us again into the Mercedes-between-motorcycles, and drove us all around Torgau and its environs. But the General was AWOL.

I shouted, "Somebody's *got* to be in charge of this operation!" We took a road west. After a long drive, the car stopped in front of a house in a village. Our host went in and came out with Capt. von Richthofen—cousin of the World War I Red Baron. The Captain spoke perfect English. He listened from the curb for about fifteen minutes to my earnest appeal. He was polite, attentive, and very sorry to inform me that there was simply nothing he could do for us. I said the matter was too important to discuss from the back seat of an automobile, and asked if there wasn't some place where we could go to give it a little more serious consideration. He suggested that both of us go for a walk.

We walked several blocks while I talked as convincingly as I could. I put a lot of emphasis on the words "futility" and "compassion." At length, he told me that he was in agreement. He said the Command realized their predicament perfectly, and that he would go talk to the Major. I waited as the Captain re-entered the house, where he stayed some twenty minutes.

When von Richthofen came out, he asked me to take another turn around town with him. He had some reservations. He thought it odd that we had gone deep into their lines when troops on the river would have done just as well. He thought it was singular that I wore cross-sabers[3] on my uniform. I asked him who else would be given a mission of working his way through enemy lines to a center where someone with enough *discrimination* and *authority* could make a *wise* decision. If not convinced, the Captain was sympathetic, and said he would do everything he could to influence the Major. He reminded me that the Major was very much an old soldier, who would have a great inner battle with his pride. Von Richthofen said that in the meantime he would personally take the matter up with the General.

Off we went again, five of us in the car, the Captain in a sidecar. We searched several villages, but no General. I hadn't known where we were, but hadn't wanted to admit it. However, as we returned to the town from which we had started, I realized it was Eilenburg. We drove to a bunker, went down and through several long passageways filled with soldiers, and into a large room with a very long table in the center lined with benches on which soldiers were sitting.

It was about 6:00 P.M. The Captain spoke several times with the Major, returning to tell me it was only a matter of the man's pride.

At about midnight, von Richthofen told me that if no decision were reached by morning he would arrange a surrender in spite of the Major. I knew that the Sixty-ninth Division was just across the Mulde on the right flank of the Timberwolves. Our bunker was near the east bank of the Mulde. I wanted both American divisions to know about the German plans to surrender. I told von Richthofen that I had to get this information across the river to the Americans right away. He asked me to write a note requesting this, and he would get the Major to approve it. The Captain came back with a *dolmacher* pass for me—signed by the Major—but kept the note.

At about three o'clock on the morning of April 25, von Richthofen told me that he had sent the note to the Major. (Later that day, I learned that he had delivered it himself and had been given an ultimatum by the Sixty-ninth to surrender by 6:00 A.M. with part of the force; the rest would remain with the Captain.) The Major would not have to do the surrendering.[4]

Von Richthofen addressed some fifty soldiers in our part of the bunker. He told them he had weighed the matter carefully both as a soldier and as a man and had come to the conclusion that it was best to surrender. He put the matter up to the men, and said they were free to act as they pleased. He referred to me several times and praised me for the "generosity" of my efforts. It was an oration, applauded several times. When he was through, every man in the audience came over and shook hands with me. They piled their weapons in a great heap on the table.

As I was leaving a latrine at exactly 6:00 A.M., artillery rounds began coming in. The soldier just ahead of me hit the ground at the same time I did. As the artillery pattern began walking south, both of us—American and German—made a dash for the bunker. The Sixty-ninth shelled Eilenburg for an hour and a half, followed by a lull.

During the lull, hysterical civilians began pouring into the bunker. They said the town was in flames. A German medic, who had been present during the Captain's oration, came into the bunker, shook his fist in my face, and told me we had shelled his hospital. He was leaving with the Major. The shelling resumed until 9:00 A.M., then ceased.

Von Richthofen and I walked to the Mulde, where German troops rose out of earthworks and foxholes along the river bank and threw their weapons into the water. We returned to the bunker and began lining up the new POWs in a column. In spite of the shelling and fires, little kids of the town came running out and followed me until I felt like the Pied Piper of Hamelin.

Within sight of the Mulde, I thought I saw something move behind one of those stone road markers. An American soldier slowly rose from behind it and said, "Jesus Christ! Are you a GI?" I answered, "Who the hell do you think I am, Betty Grable?"

Another GI appeared from the corner of a building. I told them there were some people waiting for them at the bunker, then swam the Mulde, and reported to the 104th over a field telephone and to the Sixty-ninth at First Battalion HQ. I returned to the bunker over a ladder patch on a bridge, picked up Cpl. Solowitz and the Russian, and accepted the surrender about 150 *Polizei*. The three of us disarmed the policemen and 350 German soldiers and turned them over. We brought back their pistols in two blankets, which we could scarcely carry. Von Richthofen surrendered his pistol to me, which I kept until a few years ago.

A jeep from the 104th came for us. Von Richthofen and I went back to Battalion HQ. The Colonel gave me hell for messing up his operation, and wanted to know what that German prisoner was doing in front of his CP. He took von Richthofen, denying me the right of bringing him in. When I asked why they had shelled the town, the Colonel said they had a lot of extra ammunition they wanted to use up. To add to my chagrin, I learned at Division that the Sixty-ninth had contacted the Russians that afternoon at Torgau.

I spent the next two and half hours briefing Gen. Allen and catching hell from my Old Man, Capt. Laundon. It was 1:30 on the morning of April 26. I hadn't slept since I went to bed on the night of the 22nd. I had just got back to my quarters after breakfast with the Old Man, taken off my socks, and turned on the radio when a buddy came in and told me that the Old Man wanted me to take off again. Division had picked platoon sergeant Jack Adler to try to contact the Russians at Pretzsch on the Elbe—about eighteen miles north of Torgau. Adler chose Cpl. Bob Gilfillan, Cpl. Sam Stanovich, and the same Russian to make a patrol. I was to drive them in a jeep as far as practical and then—if it appeared expedient—send the men on foot with food and instructions to hole up if necessary and wait for the Russians.

Again we left an armored car at Wellaune, drove to a point above Düben, crossed the Mulde on a hand-operated ferry, and struck out four miles east for Rösa. From Rösa, we set out for Schwemsel. Pretzsch was about twenty miles away, Berlin sixty. We had brought along a large American flag to help identify ourselves if needed. A few miles out of Schwemsel, we got the flag out, tied it to a seven-foot pole, and lashed the pole to the right side of the windshield. On the road we were bald-facedly out in the open. It seemed logical that if we could not hide. we might as well make a point of attracting attention.

Late that afternoon, we came over a rise just east of Bad Schmiedeberg. There were seven Germans astride the road with their rifles pointed at us. We lifted our helmets, stood up in the jeep, waved our hands in a friendly gesture, and drove right up to them. We could hear small-arms fire in the distance. I asked them what they were doing, and was told that they were the rear guard of a unit engaged with the Russians.

The Russians were that close.

The five of us turned east toward Pretzsch and passed the deserted village of Splau. From the brow of a hill hear Pretzsch, we saw two Russian soldiers rise to their feet from a field on our left, look carefully, then jump into the air. They, a captain, and another soldier came running over to the jeep, hugging and kissing us and chattering at the top of their voices. They piled on the fenders and hood and directed us to a ferry across the Elbe. We drove the jeep onto the ferry, and pulled it across by hand.

On the other side of the river, a phalanx of sixteen Russian soldiers gave us three rousing cheers. We drove about sixteen kilometers to the HQ of the Russian 118th Infantry Division at Annaburg. We arrived there at 7:30 P.M., April 26. We were greeted by the commanding officer, Maj. Gen. Sukhonov.

While I was talking to the General, somebody came up and put a bouquet of flowers in my hand. I wondered if this was an insinuation of effeminacy. Then someone put a bunch of lilacs in the other hand. I realized later that these people are very fond of flowers. A map was brought and I tried to show the General our location, but everything was in Russian. Eventually, we got it together and were able to exchange information. I asked for radio people, since I was a radio specialist. At first, they couldn't make anything out of our frequency system. Then they got on it, but were unable to broadcast on that wavelength.

The Russians took the five of us to dinner in a makeshift mess hall with a long table. We and Russian officers filled both sides of the table. A refined Russian captain sat next to me. He spoke good German, so we had fair communication. Toasts were made and everyone was in great spirits. The Russian captain told me that a man on a telephone was trying to tell a higher HQ about us. We were to receive decorations. (The following month, I received the Order of Alexander Nevsky at a special ceremony in Leipzig.)

The meal was macaroni and meat, salami, small raw fish, raw fat, meat covered with dough, black bread, hard-boiled eggs, hot chocolate, and cookies. Bottles of vodka had been spaced on the table at regular intervals, and half a water glass of vodka set at each place. The waiters wore light-blue tunics; every time I took a drink from my glass, the fellow from behind me would refill it. Wishing to appear equal to my Russian hosts, I kept pouring the stuff into my boot, only to have the fellow give me more.

Eventually, I got to bed in the upstairs of a farmhouse. Sometime during the night I woke up. Someone was shaking me. It was a war correspondent who wanted to know our names and addresses for a story about us.

The next morning my head was splitting. I made it to the barnyard, where men were washing. Water on my face was mercy. I had been overseas for eight months. In that land of grapes and hops, except for coffee, I had had but two drinks of plain water. That morning I not only washed in it, but even drank some.

Facing the mess hall that morning took more willpower than anything I had confronted in the past three days. When I saw bottles of vodka on the breakfast table, I knew the end had come. Even W.C. Fields once said he was a man of moderation—he never took a drink before breakfast. Yet for the honor of the U.S. Cavalry, I drank my libation. Now I know why those Russians drink so much vodka. My head cleared up, and I felt great. You have to keep drinking the stuff to stay lucid.

Leaving the mess hall, we saw that our jeep had been decorated with flowers like a Rose Festival float. The hood was covered with large bouquets of lilacs, tulips, and roses. The Russians had lashed a red flag to the left side of the jeep's windshield; it was the same size as our American flag. Our hosts had pasted newspaper pictures of Roosevelt, Churchill, and Stalin to the windshield. We started back for HQ feeling that before reaching the first German town we had best remove the adornments. Then we looked at each other, and the spirit of pride flowed unanimously through us. We took off again with flags and flowers flying. We passed long lines of German refugees moving west, carrying their few possessions, pushing carts. They stared in disbelief, then cheered us like conquering heroes. At Söllichau, the German regiment was waiting—without their colonel. He was gone. Twelve hundred men surrendered to the five of us.

On April 27, Maj. Turner (Division Artillery Air Officer) flew Col. Cochran (415th Infantry Commander), Lt. Col. Hoegh (G-3),[5] and Sgt. Sitnik (interpreter) to the Russian HQ at Annaburg. Divarty planes flew Maj. Gen. Sukhonov to our HQ at Delitzsch on April 28th. I picked up Sukhonov in my jeep at the airstrip. Gen. Allen—removing his Timberwolf patch and a safety pin from his shorts—made Sukhonov an honorary Timberwolf by pinning it on his sleeve.

Of all the experiences in my life, finding and meeting the Russians was the most memorable. When I embraced my Russian comrades that day in 1945, it would have been hard for me to believe then that one time in Palestine so many people were crucified that there was no more wood available to crucify anyone else. People have been tortured and burned alive—just to get rid of. The war made people love each other so much when it was finally over. If everyone intermingled—like we did when we linked up with the Russians—there could be no war.

H.W. ("BILL") SHANK has been an insurance agent for the past forty years.

1. HQ is the abbreviation for Headquarters.
2. A G-2 was a division intelligence officer.
3. The American cross-sabers designated military intelligence.
4. The Major, just like the Sergeant who had detained Shank earlier, may not have refused to surrender simply because of stubbornness, fanaticism, or blind loyalty. By the time Shank was captured by German soldiers, they had received orders from Berlin to fight to the last man. During the previous weeks, there had been numerous instances of local commanders hanging soldiers who merely advocated surrender.
5. A G-3 was a division operations officer.

Torgau in 1935 showing the Hartenfels Castle and the Torgau bridge. (*Manfred Bräunlich*)

Torgau town sign photographed by Paul Staub as the Robertson patrol entered the village, April 25, 1945.

Aerial view of Torgau, ca. 1935.   (*Manfred Bräunlich*)

4. JÜRGEN HERZOG

"Evacuation order received. Town will be surrendered to the Russians without a fight."

The events in and around Torgau made the world's headlines in the last days of April 1945. The Allied armies—Soviet and American soldiers—met victoriously at the Elbe. Crossing the remains of the bridge over the River Elbe at Torgau, those who had defeated Nazi fascism shook hands. The soldiers embraced each other joyfully in anticipation of the now-foreseeable end of the terrible war.

Torgau had been almost untouched by the war. Not until March 1945 had measures been taken to defend the city. The Supreme Command of the German Armed Forces had declared that all towns between the Oder and Elbe were "fortresses" to be defended against the approaching Allied armies. On March 9, residents of Torgau were ordered to erect entrenchments and defenses all around the town. The citizens subsequently constructed anti-tank blocks, field fortifications, and anti-tank trenches.

Fascist ideology was set against a background of unrest, fear, and a sense of hopelessness. In the former monastery church on a so-called "Day of Remembrance," Torgau citizens were demagogically called upon to show loyalty to Adolf Hitler. The Nazi leaders declared it was only under his leadership that the war could be won.

But as early as April 13, an order was given to evacuate all the villages in the district lying east of the Elbe. The order included Torgau itself. Under penalty of death, civilians had to leave the area. Only military units, the police, and fire fighters were permitted to remain behind.

The number of air raids on the Torgau area increased by mid-April. On April 17, an ammunition train was hit and blew up in the railway station. Two days later, large fuel tanks on the Elbe burst into flames. Even the Torgau glassworks burned down. On April 19, the residents of Torgau—old people, women, and children—left

41

the town on foot and on bicycles. The refugees were loaded down with only the most necessary baggage. Many pushed handcarts. All were looking for shelter in the villages west of the Elbe.

I was four years old at the time. I remember leaving Torgau with my mother and three-month-old sister. My mother pushed my sister in a baby carriage. With hardly any luggage at all, we left the town on a trailer pulled by a tractor. My grandparents left Torgau on bicycles. Because my father was missing and my uncle had been killed, my grandfather took it upon himself to look after my grandmother, mother, aunt, and us children.

It was a new adventure for me. The stream of fleeing, frightened people. The village where we sought refuge. And I running for a ditch as soon as an airplane appeared on the horizon.

On April 24, the situation in Torgau came to a head. Would the town itself be destroyed, or would the commanding officer surrender it? At approximately noon, Soviet artillery opened fire on the town from the east bank of the river. The fire department worked around the clock putting out fires.

> Many sisters lost their brothers,
> Wives widowed by the war.
> Amid the fire and desolation
> Children found families no more.
>
> Yes, hungry children there wandered,
> Wandered the highways in little bands,
> Met other children, who joined them there
> Amid the ruined towns and lands.
>
> They wanted to escape the slaughter,
> The nightmare to cease,
> And one day find a country
> Where at last there would be peace.
>
> A girl of eleven that day
> Carried a child of four.
> She was a mother in every way
> Seeking a country without war.
>
> BERTOLT BRECHT

On the night of April 24, the commanding officer decided to surrender, and ordered the military units still in Torgau—around the bridge and along the Elbe—to retreat. At 2:15 a.m. on April 25, fire officials noted in the department records:

> Evacuation order received. Town will be surrendered to the Russians without a fight. Everyone to move to the southwest part of the district.

The Elbe bridge, the harbor bridge, and several small bridges around Torgau were blown up by order of the commanding officer. The explosions took place at approximately 3:30 a.m. The powerful detonations, which caused unnecessary destruction, announced the withdrawal of the fascist troops. The town was deserted—Torgau was a no man's land. But it had escaped devastation!

Those in the bunker of the Reich Chancellery in Berlin followed the approach of the Allied forces with apprehension. The fascist leaders never gave up hope, even up until the last minute. They were hoping for a surprise encounter between the western and eastern fronts, followed by armed clashes between the Allied forces themselves which would result in a rapid disintegration of the alliance.

But it did not work out that way. On April 25 at about 4:00 p.m., a jeep driven by Second Lt. William Robertson, a twenty-year-old American soldier, raced through the deserted streets of Torgau. Robertson sent a message from the castle tower to the Red Army soldiers on the east bank of the river. On the girders of the ruined Elbe bridge, American and Soviet soldiers shook hands.

Their handshake meant victory. The long-awaited end of the war had come.

DR. JÜRGEN HERZOG is Assistant Manager of the Flachglas Kombinat Torgau and Chairman of the League of Culture's working group on local history.

5. Heinz Blüthchen

"Powerful detonations cut into the air, breaking the Torgau bridge, plunging it into the waters of the Elbe."

April 1945. By the middle of the month, there is growing unrest among the populace of Torgau. We can hear the noise of battle as the fronts are closing in on the town. Soviet units from the east and American troops from the west are advancing to the Elbe. Anxiously, the people of Torgau await the end of the war.

The broad arches of the railway bridge are still spanning the Elbe—the Nazi troops have not as yet given the order to blow it up. The townspeople hope against hope that the bridge will remain intact.

Rumors are everywhere. The Soviet Army has already reached the approaches of the Elbe. The anxious waiting for us all will soon be coming to an end. Then the Nazis give us the order:

"All communities as far as Torgau are to be evacuated in preparation for battles to come."

Hurriedly, people throughout the evacuation area gather their belongings. They rush panic-stricken to the train station. They're pushing handcarts, they're loaded down with backpacks, they're carrying baskets in which they've placed their most necessary possessions. They want to bet on board—*now*. This might be the last train going west.

The train compartments are filled to overflowing. Men and women are fighting for a place, even on the ledges between cars, even on the engine itself. They have one thought alone—get away. It's a matter of life and death. Get away. The Nazi commanders couldn't care less if women, children, and the elderly are killed in the final moments of the war. Yes, get away.

The beaming spring sun, as if in mockery, is bathing this sorry scene with a glistening light. Blinded by the brightness, the engineer lets his eyes wander along the railway track as the train is approaching Torgau. Pale and anxious, the stoker August Schäfer rushes up to him.

"Did you see it, Rieback?" he stammers, tapping the engineer on the shoulder, and pointing to the nearby woods where shells are exploding, making a terrifying noise. The bridge flashes through the engineer's mind. The railway bridge. Has it already been blown up?

Engineer Rieback accelerates the locomotive. The overloaded train creaks forward. Then relief—the bridge is yet undamaged. It's over this bridge that hundreds of refugees are making their way out of hell.

Troubled days pass. Finally, the Nazi commander of Torgau gives the order to evacuate the town—completely. Lunatic military strategists want to continue defending Torgau to the last, even though the outcome of the war has already been decided. From opposite directions, the Allied armies are closing in. It might be just a matter of hours before American and Soviet soldiers meet. It's still dark outside, but day is breaking in the east. Then sirens suddenly begin to wail, striking fear in the hearts of those still remaining in Torgau.

On the night of April 24, powerful detonations cut into the air, breaking the Torgau bridge, plunging it into the waters of the Elbe. The fascist army's demolition squad has done their deadly job. Just before their retreat, they separated both river banks. This was the final evil act which the fanatical followers of the Nazi regime perpetrated in our town.

A few hours later, American and Soviet soldiers shook hands on the banks of the Elbe. This marked the end of a terrible war.

HEINZ BLÜTHCHEN, former Chief Engineer for the reconstruction of the Torgau railway bridge, lives in Torgau.

6. BILL ROBERTSON

"About halfway across the Elbe, the Russian soldier and I slid down a huge 'V' formed by the bent girder."

(Photo courtesy Bill Robertson)

An exhausted Bill Robertson being interviewed on the morning of April 26, 1945.

After the Sixty-ninth Division captured Leipzig in April 1945, it continued to advance eastward. My own regiment, the 273rd, reached the Mulde River on about April 20. Every GI knew that the Russians were headed in our direction. We knew the ultimate defeat of Nazi Germany was now certain. But when that would happen, how many of us would survive—these were the pressing questions.

Our orders were to stop at the Mulde. No reconnaissance missions were to be made east of the river. Higher authority then decided that American patrols could go east of the Mulde, but no farther than five miles.

I was a Second Lt., S-2 (Reconnaissance) officer of our battalion. I commanded a small squad. Our regiment was bivouacked on the Mulde just across from the town of Wurzen. On April 24, the *bürgermeister* crossed to the west bank of the river and surrendered to us. We subsequently moved into Wurzen. My own squad was very busy that night setting up a POW enclosure and checking the area.

By that time, the possibility of meeting the Soviet army had become the sole topic of conversation. All of us were filled with curiosity and anticipation. We wondered what the Russians were doing. Who were they? We knew that they had fought all the way from Stalingrad, from Moscow, that they were tough soldiers. But what were they *really* like? How did they act? Were they friendly or not? All we knew was that they were in front of us—out there somewhere. And we realized that it would be a great honor for the Sixty-ninth Division to be the first unit of the Western front to link up with the Eastern front.

Soon after we entered Wurzen, we discovered a *stalag* (POW camp) just four miles east of the town. Some four thousand ex-POWs straggled in from the camp. Although weak and emaciated, they greeted us with joy shining in their eyes. I was impressed by how much they personified the global aspect of the war. Some had been captured in the North African Campaign. Many were Russians, Poles, Frenchmen, Englishmen, Canadians, Indians, Australians, as well as Americans. Their happiness was indescribable— their eyes followed us as if they couldn't get enough.

The liberated POWs entering Wurzen were soon joined by hundreds of refugees and forced laborers newly freed. There were Poles, Serbs, Czechs, Frenchmen, and other nationalities. Growing numbers of German civilians began arriving on foot, on bicycles, pushing or pulling carts piled high with belongings.

Even though the morning of April 25 was clear, our own situation was not. The Sixty-ninth was setting up tents and field kitchens on the west bank of the Mulde for the ex-POWs and the refugees. German soldiers began surrendering, entering the town in both small and large groups. The crew of a self-propelled 88 millimeter gun mounted on a Panther tank chassis surrendered the weapon to us intact.

On that morning, I was given a mission by Battalion Headquarters. My instructions were to survey the roads leading into Wurzen to get a rough idea of how many refugees were coming into town. This would enable the Sixty-ninth to make adequate provisions for food and shelter. I was further instructed to plan and guard POW enclosures. I picked three men of our Recon section: Cpl. James McDonnell of Peabody, Massachusetts; Pfc. Frank Huff of Washington, Virginia; and Pfc. Paul Staub of the Bronx, New York (Paul spoke German).

The four of us got into our jeep, equipped with a machine gun. But we had neither flares nor a radio. The patrol drove east a couple of miles, saw only a few refugees, and urged them on to Wurzen. We returned to town, and at about 10:00 A.M. took another road leading northeast. On this road we found many refugees whom we again urged to hurry along. We continued to move up the road.

This, then, was the beginning of the patrol that eventually ended up some twenty miles away in Torgau, the patrol which was the second one to contact the Soviet army. When we first left Wurzen, we had no intention of going to Torgau, located quite a distance from us in enemy territory. We had no intention of meeting the Russians. Although armed with a machine gun, we were only one jeep strong—certainly no "motorized patrol."

Driving northeast, the four of us accepted the surrender of a German rifle company of about three hundred men plus officers. I had them stack their rifles and break the stocks. We confiscated their side arms, and wrote out a "safe-conduct" pass to Wurzen. We then chased and stopped a German staff car, found it full of medical officers, and sent them back to Wurzen.

The patrol proceeded carefully because I felt that at some point we would encounter rear-echelon German troops—a quartermaster supply depot, field hospital, kitchens, or whatever. We captured two SS men who offered minor resistance, disarmed them, and seated them on the hood of the jeep.

Nearing Torgau, the patrol came upon a small group of English POWs who had escaped from the town and were making their way for the American lines. They told us of some wounded Yanks in a Torgau prison camp. At that point, I decided to continue to Torgau if we could. Up until then, we had encountered no fire except for shots from the SS men, who now sat sullenly on the hood of the jeep.

Approaching Torgau, we saw smoke coming from a few fires presumably caused by previous Russian artillery barrage. We reconnoitered the southern outskirts of the town. The four of us now felt quite exposed, as we had no means of identification except our uniforms. We didn't have any green flares—the prearranged signal of the Americans to the Russians. So we confiscated a white bed sheet from a German civilian we met on the road, tore out about a five-by-eight foot section, tied it to a stick, rolled it up, and tossed it into the back of the jeep. We thought the Russians might not shoot at us if we met them waving a white flag.

When our patrol reached Torgau at 1:30 P.M., it was a ghost town. I don't believe I saw more than forty German civilians the whole time we were there. In Torgau, we came across the small prison camp at Fort Zinna the Tommies had told us about. It held about forty men, all sentenced to death for espionage. We found two wounded GIs who had been captured only a few days earlier. They were being treated by a Yugoslav doctor. We promised help soon.

Small-arms fire sounded to the east, toward the Elbe. Leaving the two SS men at the prison camp, we drove in the direction of the firing. Our patrol soon met a German civilian, who told Paul that the Soviet army was on the other side of the river.

We decided to attempt contact. The time was about 2:00 P.M.

The patrol then encountered some sniper fire in town. We left the jeep, spread out, and detoured around the snipers. By now, the two Americans from the prison camp had joined us. We were a patrol of six.

Because we were planning to contact the Russians who were on the other side of the Elbe, I felt we needed better identification. The six of us broke into the first drug store (apothecary) we saw and found some colored powders—red and blue. We mixed the powders with water, and painted our bed sheet with five horizontal red stripes and a field of blue in the upper left corner. The time was 3:00 P.M.

We moved cautiously toward the river. I looked for some tall building or tower from which to wave the flag. Then we saw Hartenfels Castle. It had a magnificent tower very close to the west bank of the Elbe.

The castle had one entrance through a walled courtyard. I went in with Jim McDonnell, Paul Staub, and Ensign George Peck—one of the two liberated American POWs. I left Frank Huff and the other ex-POW with the jeep.

The four of us climbed the circular staircase inside the tower. Leaving the three men on the upper landing, I crawled out at roof level, waved the flag so that the Russians could see it, and began shouting *"Amerikanski"* and *"Tovarisch."* The time was about 3:30.

The firing stopped.

Russian soldiers were about five to six hundred yards away—

across the river, then some two hundred yards beyond on a sloping grass embankment. They were moving about in the cover of trees at the edge of some woods.

They shouted. I could not understand.

I shouted. They could not understand.

They then fired two *green* flares (not *red!*). I couldn't respond, since we didn't have any flares. They then opened fire again, this time not just at the tower, but at the whole town as well. While this was going on, German snipers were firing at me from the rear.

I then waved our American flag, trying to stay under cover as much as possible. I shouted *"Amerikanski"* and *"Tovarisch"* over and over, explaining in English that we were an American patrol.

They ceased firing and started shouting again. I hung the flag pole out of the tower at a right angle so that they could easily see the stripes. By this time, I had sent the jeep back to the prison camp to find a Russian POW who could speak German.

The Russians resumed firing. This time, though, an anti-tank gun coughed from the left side of the woods (I could see the smoke). The round hit the tower about five to six feet from me.

Again, they stopped firing.

The jeep brought a liberated Russian POW from the prison camp. Paul hurriedly explained to him in German what to tell his countrymen across the river. The Russian leaned out of the tower and shouted a few sentences.

All firing ceased.

A small group of Russian soldiers started walking toward the river bank.

We left the tower, ran through the courtyard, and raced to the river. A road bridge stood near the castle. It had been blown up, probably by the retreating German army. Although the girders were bent and twisted, one of them was still above water level. We could see no boats on our side of the Elbe.

I started for the bridge, but the liberated Russian POW got there first. He started across the girder. A Russian soldier on the east bank began crawling on the girder toward us. Following the Russian POW, I climbed, then slid along the girder. Right behind me were Ensign Peck and Frank Huff. The rest of the patrol remained with the jeep. Paul was even taking pictures of us.

The POW met the soldier, passed him, and continued to the east bank while his countryman continued toward us. About halfway across the Elbe, the Russian soldier and I slid down a limb of a huge "V" formed by the bent girder. The symbolism is interesting, since "V" was the sign for Victory. But we didn't think of that at the time.

The Russian was Sgt. Nikolai Andreyev. We shook hands and carefully pounded each other on the shoulder, trying not to fall into the swift current below. The time was four o'clock.

The Russian continued moving along the girder to the west bank. We continued to the east, where we were met by soldiers greeting us with happy yells. More soldiers were arriving by the minute.

The time was 4:45. We three Americans were standing with the Russians on the river bank laughing, shouting, pounding each other on the back, shaking hands with everyone. Frank, George, and I were shouting in English, our hosts in Russian. Neither understood the other's words, but the commonality of feeling was unmistakable. We were all soldiers, comrades in arms. We had vanquished a common enemy. The war was over, peace was near. All of us would live for another hour, another day.

The celebration continued as more Russians arrived. One produced a box of captured rations—sardines, biscuits, canned meat, chocolate. Wine and schnapps appeared. We toasted each other. We toasted the end of the war. We toasted the United States, the Soviet Union, and our Allies. We toasted our commanders and national leaders.

We gazed at each other with open curiosity. The Russian soldiers seemed quite young, but I guess we were too. They looked like any other combat soldier I'd ever seen, but were cleaner than many. They wore their decorations on their combat uniforms, but didn't wear steel helmets—I don't know why. Several had continued fighting at the front in spite of bandages on their wounds. I was surprised to see such a motley group of pleasant-faced, jolly fellows. We traded souvenirs such as cap ornaments and insignia. I traded wrist watches with a Russian captain who had been wounded five times since Stalingrad. One soldier gave me his gold wedding band.

A Russian major who spoke English then arrived. I suggested we should make arrangements for our respective regimental and division commanders to meet at Torgau the following day at 10:00 A.M. I told him I had to return to our lines. The Major informed me that our patrol had made contact with elements of the Fifty-eighth "Garde" Division of the First Ukrainian Army, commanded by Marshal Konyev. "Garde" meant that it was a "crack" division cited for bravery in the Battle of Stalingrad.

It was getting late, and I wanted to return to Wurzen before dark. I asked for a liaison group to go with us. Four Russians volunteered. They were Maj. Anafim Larionov, Capt. Vasily Nyeda, Lt. Alexander Silvashko (commander of the platoon at the bridge), and Sgt. Nikolai Andreyev, whom I had met first on the Torgau bridge.

At five o'clock, we re-crossed the Elbe in a racing shell the Russians had found. The eight of us climbed into the jeep and retraced our route. By dusk, we had arrived without incident in Wurzen. At First Battalion HQ, there was more handshaking, celebrating, and toasting when it was announced that these were Russian troops, that a linkup had occurred. Photographers were there taking pictures of all of us standing on the steps of the CP.

Suddenly, a shot rang out.

A German civilian who had been standing nearby fell to the ground—the top of his head blown off. As blood spurted from the severed carotid arteries, he lay on the sidewalk kicking.

What had happened? We were told that he had been picked up earlier on suspicion of being a leader of the Werewolf organization and of serving as a prison guard at Fort Zinna. He had not as yet been checked by his American captors. But when he saw the four Russians at the CP, he thought his time had come. As everyone was celebrating, he had grabbed an M1 from the shoulder of a GI, put the muzzle under his chin, and pulled the trigger.

Not long after this incident, we proceeded to Regimental CP at Trebsen. Regiment had already been notified of the linkup. Col. Charles Adams, commander of the 273rd, welcomed the Russian delegation. The reception for my own patrol was a lot less certain, since we had ventured well beyond the five-mile limit. Although we didn't know it at the time, Col. Adams had two other patrols out beyond the limit. The Colonel had already been chewed out at Division by Gen. Reinhardt, commander of the 69th.

A much larger party then joined us as we drove to Division HQ at Naunhof. Gen. Reinhardt welcomed the Russians, but ordered the Robertson Patrol to be locked up in the G-3's office. There was talk of court-martialing us, since we had disobeyed orders by going far beyond the five-mile limit. We were in hot water.

But the Power and Presence of the Press are remarkable. Word had gotten around the First Army's Press Camp that the Sixty-ninth Division, at the leading edge of the First Army's lines, might soon make contact with the Russian front. Correspondents and news photographers were thick around Division HQ. They *knew* something was happening.

Reinhardt notified Gen. Huebner of V Corps of our linkup. Gen. Huebner berated Gen. Reinhardt, then notified Gen. Hodges of the First Army. Gen. Hodges was awakened at about midnight with the report that the Robertson Patrol had met the Russians and that a Russian delegation was right then at Division CP.

What was Gen. Hodges's reaction? He said he was "delighted" with the news. He told Gen. Huebner to *congratulate* Gen. Reinhardt. All was forgiven.

The Robertson Patrol and the Russians were then introduced to a mob of reporters. The news was out. Pictures were taken, including the AP photo of Lt. Silvashko and me which appeared on the front pages of newspapers around the world. The Press then left to file their stories and return for the next day's meetings.

By then, it was past midnight. The date was April 26. Our patrol was very tired, having gotten little sleep the night before. The Russians had to get back to their lines. We had made arrangements for our COs to meet at ten o'clock that morning in Torgau. So back we went to Regiment to organize a fourteen-jeep patrol.

Since the four of us already knew the way to Torgau, our jeep led the convoy. This patrol, accompanied by Col. Adams, arrived in Torgau at dawn. The Press also arrived. It was on the 26th that most of the picture of the Torgau linkup were taken, including the movie footage.

On the 26th, we learned that Lt. Albert Kotzebue's twenty-eight man jeep patrol from our 273rd Regiment had actually been the first to meet the Russians. Buck Kotzebue's patrol had also met part of the Fifty-eighth "Garde" Division. They made contact the previous day at Strehla, located on the Elbe about sixteen miles south of Torgau. Kotzebue had met the Russians at 12:30 P.M.— three and a half hours before we did. The Kotzebue Patrol therefore deserves credit for being the *first* American unit to link up with the Russians.

When the Robertson Patrol returned with the Russian delegation to the U.S. lines on the evening of April 25, we had met the Press without much delay. The news was flashed to the world. We got most of the publicity, as well as the credit for the first "official" linkup, the linkup in Torgau. In the meantime, however, Buck and his men remained in the Russian lines overnight. He was not able to make contact with Division, let alone the Press, until after the "official" meetings at Torgau.

DR. WILLIAM D. ROBERTSON returned from the war to pursue medical studies in California. After completion of Neurological Residency in Great Britain and the United States, Dr. Robertson practiced neurosurgery in the Los Angeles area. He retired in 1984.

(National Archives)

Robertson and Huff with their replica of the American flag, in Torgau, Germany. George Peck had earlier torn the right corner from the flag to prove in later years "that this whole experience was not a dream."

(*Source: Bill Robertson*)

Col. Charles Adams, commander of the US 273rd Regiment, leads American and Soviet soldiers in a victory toast at regimental headquarters at Trebsen. *From left:* Lt. Alexander Silvashko, Maj. Anafim Larionov, Col. Adams, Sgt. Nikolai Andreyev (whom Robertson first met on the Torgau roadbridge), and Robertson.

(*Paul Staub*)

Robertson Patrol at the Elbe River on the afternoon of April 25, 1945. *From left:* Pfc. Frank Huff, Cpl. James McDonnell, Lt. Bill Robertson, and Pfc. Paul Staub.

7. GEORGE PECK

"We waved frantically and started running for the bridge."

On the afternoon of April 25, 1945, Sgt. Victor Berruti and I were sitting by the side of a road near Torgau, not far from Fort Zinna. Looking down the road, we caught a glimpse of a lone jeep disappearing around a bend.

"Looks like they're going away, Lieutenant," Victor remarked.

"Maybe they'll come back," I replied. "Let's sit here and wait for them."

Victor and I were liberated on that April day. On October 13, 1944, five of us Americans from the OSS had been captured near Turin, Italy, after a day long shoot-out high in the Alps. My German captors had found it hard to understand what I, a naval ensign, was doing at an altitude of nine thousand feet. But when they found out that we were in the intelligence service, they got the picture.

Our group was shipped off to Germany—well out of reach of the Italian partisans who had tried to free us. On November 9, I escaped from jail in the Bavarian town of Moosburg, only to be recaptured four days later. This escapade did little to endear me to my captors. It led to my being confined to solitary for almost five months—a lesson in patience. On about April 1, my companions and I were transferred to Fort Zinna. At that time, it was the only large military prison still operating in Nazi Germany. There, we were to stand trial as spies.

When we arrived at Fort Zinna, the Germans took us to a sort of outer office, where we were processed. A trusty of doubtful appearance stealthily approached us. He pointed to a stack of

56

folders lying on a counter top. Each was marked with a large "T". Those, he said, were our dossiers, and added:

" *'T' meint Tod!*" (" 'D' means death!")

Fear fell upon us.

I was again separated from my companions. That evening, at nightfall, I could hear sounds coming from across the fields, sounds resembling small sticks being snapped in half. I heard them again, then realized that the firing squad was at work—a nightly event at Fort Zinna. Meditating in the gathering gloom, I realized that if God meant me to continue on earth, that would be all right too. A great sense of peacefulness came over me as I thought, "Thou preservest him in perfect peace whose mind is stayed on Thee."

About an hour later, I had a visitor. André Levacher, a French captain, seemed an angel of mercy. He said he knew all about our case. André told me not to worry, predicting that the Nazi military judges would not press the charges of espionage against us when they themselves were likely to be in the dock in the near future. And so indeed it turned out.

As he left my cell, André asked if I would like to be transferred to his cell, which he shared with Bertelsen, the Danish ex-Consul General. Would I! The next day, I moved in with them; we talked non-stop for twelve hours. André lived in Châlons-sur-Marne, and had seen his home destroyed twice—in 1914 and 1940. His crime was that after having been captured with the whole army on the Maginot Line, he had operated an underground railroad for escaped French POWs. Bertelsen was reticent about his own connections with the British underground, as his case was still pending. His contributions to the conversation consisted of witty good humor and the passing on of many goodies sent down from Berlin by the Danish Foreign Office. He gave me four hundred cigarettes with which I bought an excellent Swiss-made German army watch.

One prominent German prisoner who frequently visited our cell was Gen. Oskar Ritter von Niedermayer, a scion of the Bavarian nobility and former chief of the *Wehrpolitisches Institut* in Berlin. As the American and Russian armies were advancing toward us from opposite directions, the General gladly shared his expert knowledge of military strategy with André, who in some ways was becoming the unofficial head of the prison.

Like von Niedermayer, most of the two thousand or so prisoners bulletins in the *Völkischer Beobachter,* we knew by April 20 that the Russians were stalled two miles east of us across the Elbe, and the Americans twenty or so miles to the west on the banks of the Mulde.

When the front drew near, a field hospital moved in, filling the cellars of the fort with wounded soldiers. On April 23, orders came through to evacuate the fort. All were to withdraw with the remaining German forces to Bavaria, where the Nazis were to make a last stand in the so-called *Festung Europa.* The next day, André told the prison authorities that they could do what they pleased with the German prisoners, but that the Allied POWs and wounded would not leave. To my surprise, the authorities agreed. The German prisoners departed on the evening of the 24th, leaving the fort in the hands of the French, British, Russians, Italians, and us.

April 25, the great day, dawned in a cold drizzle. Up betimes to test our new freedom, we gathered in the front courtyard of the prison. There we witnessed a heart-rending scene which might have come straight out of the Thirty Years War—that other great German tragedy.

The Nazis were evacuating the field hospital. Ambulatory patients were hobbling along, some scantily clad and wrapped in blankets, others practically barefooted. The more seriously-wounded were riding in commandeered farm wagons, the kind usually used to cart potatoes or manure. The wounded lying in the wagons were mercilessly joggled as the horses pulled the carts over the cobblestones.

Several of us approached the Nazi medical officer-in-charge and asked him to leave the badly-wounded Germans behind as an act of mercy. Of course, his job was to repair the broken bodies so that they could again serve as *Kannonenfutter,* but that was not his answer. He turned violently on us and launched into an invective which ended with the prediction, "In two months, we will push you Americans back into the North Sea!"

We thought he was crazy. Finally, the last cart passed through the gate of the ancient fortress. On its tailgate sat a Red Cross nurse with her feet dangling over the board. I saw tears streaming down her plain, German face.

André was in charge of the fort now. One of the first things he did was post a guard at the wine cellar of the fortress. He with her feet dangling over the board. I saw tears streaming down her plain, German face.

André was in charge of the fort now. One of the first things he did was post a guard at the wine cellar of the fortress. He maintained that the wine, most of which was French, was by right ours. However, he didn't act fast enough to frustrate a very large and very wild Irishman in the British service, who got a skinfull by 8:00 A.M. Paddy started breaking up the furniture and making a great row. We didn't know what to do until our staunch American sergeant, Victor Berruti, showed up. Victor never let us down in a pinch. He wheedled Paddy toward the entrance of Cell Block D, threw open the gate, and offered him any room in the house. Soothed by his amiable ruse, Paddy progressed into the lachrymose stage and submitted to being led to a bunk to sleep it off.

Like Paddy, each of us explored the joys of freedom in his own way. In addition to running the fortress, André led the French contingent in the preparation of a glorious celebration feast. The Russian lieutenant—the pilot Titov—had worked in the poultry yard up until our liberation; he contributed dozens of eggs and a supply of young spring chickens. The English captain, Lewis Lee-Graham, had miraculously survived years of severe malnutrition, pneumonia, and the bombing of his prison; he wanted a good, long, hot bath—and got it. The Italian colonel reasserted his tarnished authority by having his enlisted men black his boots.

As for me, I was seized by a fear of anarchy. Because the Germans had left a vacuum in authority, I felt called upon to fill it. I asked André if I could see to the comfort of the Allied wounded. Readily agreeing, he lent me a smartly-cut French jacket to replace my worn GI overcoat. I now looked more like an officer. Victor found a silver bar to pin on my overseas cap. The illusion was effective, if perhaps confusing. The wounded—forty or so Russians and a handful of Americans—were carefully brought up from the cellar and installed in clean beds in an airy barracks.

Shortly after noon, someone rushed into the fortress with the electrifying news, "The Americans are here!" But it was a false report. Victor and I became impatient, and so went out at about three o'clock to look for the Americans. A warm sun had come out by the time we sat down by the road. The chestnut trees were just coming into bloom. And we were glad to be out on our own.

We sat down on the side of the road. It was long, straight, flat.

It led across the plain to the west and—we hoped—to the Americans. We waited.

At 3:15 P.M., we spotted a tiny vehicle at the point where the road centered its lines of perspective on the horizon. As the spot grew larger, we saw that it was a jeep. The back seat was full of small arms. On the pile perched a GI corporal.

"Hiya, fellas!" he called out. Never have the accents of my native New York sounded sweeter. Like Victor, he was from the East Bronx. The two were soon in deep conversation about home addresses, delicatessens, and restaurants—food was an obsession with both POWs and GIs.

The commander of the patrol was Second Lt. William Robertson, who introduced himself as "Bill." He was from Los Angeles, and right now had more serious concerns on his mind.

"Are there any Germans in Torgau?" he asked.

"No," I answered, eager to be of service. "They pulled out this morning at about seven. But there may be a few *Volkssturm* around." The *Volkssturm* was that pitiable militia of old men and boys who were supposed to defend their homes.

"Where are the Russians?" Bill asked.

"At Brückenkopf, just across the river," we answered. "They came about two days ago and have stayed there."

"Let's see if we can find them!" Bill said.

Robertson admitted that he was not supposed to be there at all. His patrol had run ahead of the American lines, enticed by the great number of Germans who were anxious to give up their arms to the Americans instead of to the dreaded Russians. Hence, the pile of pistols, machine pistols, and tommy guns on the back seat of the jeep.

Bill gave us our pick of weapons, and invited us to join the patrol. The six of us drove on into Torgau itself. Bill then got out of the jeep and led four of us in echelon formation on each side of the street; Victor followed in the jeep. Here and there, a house was quietly on fire. No one took notice.

We came out onto the marketplace. Bill had a large white sheet which he planned to use as a flag whenever we got to the Russians. Victor and I said that this was not such a good idea, as the Germans had been overdoing that tactic recently, and the Russians would certainly take us for Germans. Someone said, "Let's paint it so it will look like an American flag."

This said, Bill went up to a hardware store, shot out the lock and pane of glass with his machine gun, and reached through to undo the latch. We found dry water paint, mixed up the colors, made three broad red stripes across the sheet, and painted a blue field in one corner. The spots where the blue paint didn't stick were meant to be stars. It was quite a flag; I had taken the precaution of tearing a corner from it to show doubting persons as proof that this whole experience was not a dream. Later, we heard, Bill gave it to Gen. Eisenhower, who is said to have passed it on to the Smithsonian—the nation's attic.

Coming out of the store, we found our way to Hartenfels Castle, right across the river from the Russian lines. The castle was a fortress built by Frederick the Great of Prussia in the 1740s after his victory over Saxony and Austria. It had a watchtower with a platform surmounted by a crown-shaped dome.

Having driven through the courtyard entrance to the castle, we raced up the stairs and came out high above the river, swirling below. The bridge had been blown up; the roadway was totally destroyed, with only the twisted girders of the superstructure remaining. On the far side of the Elbe—about five hundred yards away—were the Russian lines. They had erected a series of earthworks running in front of the small military prison of Brückenkopf. A Russian armored truck stood in the lee of one of the few houses. Lying between the Russians and us were a wide, green field, the river with two web-like bridges spanning it, and the Torgau embankment.

We could see figures walking around behind the earthworks.

Briefly surveying the situation, Bill clambered up a rickety ladder in the belfry through a trap door to the open space under the dome. He climbed up over the platform onto the dome—more than a hundred feet above the Elbe—and began precariously waving the flag at the Russians.

No response.

I called up, "Shout *Amerikanskii soldatui!*" I had dreamed many times in the prison of being liberated by the Russians, and had got hold of a German Russian Soldier's Dictionary. I had learned all the expressions in the front of the book, especially words such as *drug* ("friend"), *daitye mnye khlyeb* ("give me bread"), *gyde . . . ?* (where is . . . ?"), etc.

Robertson was getting results. We could see heads peep out from behind the earthworks.

Then a red flare went up.

"Damn it!" Bill shouted, "I forgot the flare." (American patrols were supposed to carry answering green flares in case they met the Russians.)

From our side of the Elbe, scattered *Volkssturm* fired a few sniper shots. This was enough for the Russians. They opened fire.

It was very impressive. The entire line blossomed with flashes of flame. From where we were, it looked like striking flints. The sparks mushroomed out; I could look down the middle to see the bullet coming.

We all ducked. But not Bill. He kept waving the flag. After a while, he got tired, and came down to the platform.

"Look," I told him, "I've got a friend at the fort, a Lt. Titov, who's a Russian pilot shot down over Stalingrad. He can talk to them in Russian."

Bill yelled down to Victor—still in the jeep—to high-tail it back to Fort Zinna and bring back the Russian lieutenant. After an interminable wait, the jeep reappeared, and Titov came puffing up the stairs. I began explaining the situation to him in German, which he did not understand very well. But Victor must have gotten the message across to him, for the pilot sprang into the belfry and began yelling at the top of his large lungs in Russian, drawing out his syllables in long, mournful cries. I thanked our lucky stars that he was a husky fellow—in civilian life a hunter from Vladivostok—because he must have had to bellow for five minutes.

A few heads reappeared on the east bank. Soldiers began coming out from behind trees, out of shallow trenches. Titov must have been asking them to come down to the river. A few jumped over the earthworks.

Bill shouted, "Let's go!" and we all scrambled down the stairs, jumped into the jeep, and sped up onto the embankment.

The opposite fields were filling up with soldiers. We waved frantically and started running for the bridge. I asked Bill if I might come along with him, since I knew German and they might not have someone who knew English.

But Bill was already crawling on the twisted girders of the bridge. I followed close behind. A Russian sergeant had already got a good start toward us from the other bank. He met Bill, and

And then I edged by. The girder was not wide; it was not easy to manage without falling into the rushing river below. But we made our way to the east bank, where we were greeted by a group of Russians. All of us were jabbering, shaking hands, and slapping each other on the backs.

We asked the Russians where they had come from, and they answered, "Stalingrad." Theirs was a unit of the Ukrainian army; they looked as though they had walked the whole way. There were almost no vehicles anywhere, except one truck and a few liberated horse wagons—so different from our own highly-mechanized forces. I was also surprised by their uniforms. Although ours were not exactly colorful, theirs seemed drab. They all wore frayed outfits, all but the commanding officer—a smartly uniformed major. A tall blond, he looked like Alexander Nevsky—the real one, not the actor who played the part in the Eisenstein film.

Bill and the Major sat down to exchange credentials and talk. I offered to serve as interpreter, since the *lingua franca* in this part of Europe was not English—as it is now—but German. The Major fixed a hard stare on me and barked, "*Nyet!*" I had forgotten the Russian attitude, which was that any POW was considered a treacherous deserter until proven otherwise.

As the two talked, I noticed another important difference between our armies—there were a number of women here dressed just like the men. They were paramedics. I had once known a Russian paramedic just like them who had been taken prisoner by the Germans. The job of these women was to administer first aid, no matter how hazardous the fighting. Many were killed in battle. I found out later that the proportion of battle-wounded who were saved was higher in the Russian army than in any other, including our own.

By this time, the celebration had gotten under way. One Russian soldier was firing a German bazooka into the river; the missile made a big splash and satisfying bang. The Russians passed around German schnapps, as well as German cheese, sausage, bread, and chocolate. In the absence of much verbal communication, there was a lot of hugging and backslapping.

A Russian captain befriended me. His chest was covered with well-worn medals—not just the ribbons, but the whole medals. This heroic figure gave me a big hug, but it developed that he was not especially attracted to me, but to my 400-cigarette watch. The historic occasion, he said, should be memorialized by our exchanging watches, and he offered me a woman's brass watch that was no longer working. He said my wife would like it, I was so astonished that I reluctantly agreed, and was left with the thought that this shrewd fellow enjoyed historic occasions to his own advantage.

Sitting there in the light of the westering sun, I had time for reflection. This was indeed an historic occasion. For another person, I suppose, this mood would have seemed incongruous amid all the rejoicing. But I was an historian, one who had been deeply involved in political intelligence for several years. That afternoon, sitting on the banks of the Elbe, I remembered that the Spanish Civil War, in which other "premature anti-fascists" like me had fought, had started nearly ten years earlier. The long struggle against the fascist dictatorships was finally coming to a close. Britain was saved. So too were France and Italy, though starved and battered. Jewish survivors of the death camps were being freed.

I was suddenly flooded with a warm surge of hope. That same day, the United Nations was being formed in San Francisco. The peace of the world was to be founded upon the friendship of our two great nations—the United States and Soviet Union.

Bill and the Major concluded their business; they arranged a meeting between their commanding officers, a meeting which took place the next day on a bridge farther down the river. "I've got to get back to the Mulde before sundown," Bill suddenly said. "It's nearly five. Let's get going!"

A Russian soldier discovered an abandoned motor launch by the river and jumped in. But because the motor wouldn't start, another soldier found a rowboat to ferry us across. On the west bank, we were joined by a Russian medical contingent, which followed us to Fort Zinna. They immediately evacuated the Russian wounded, leaving the Americans with us. Bill left Victor and me there, saying he would report our whereabouts. Help would arrive by morning, which it did.

The Russians didn't leave us right away. One of them came up to André and pointed to a seventeen-year-old German boy wearing an SS uniform. The Russian indicated by sign language that he wanted to shoot him. André well knew of the horrors of National Socialism. He knew the barbarous acts committed by the SS not only in the Soviet Union, but also in his own country. Yet he refused to surrender the young German. Instead, he sent the boy home—to his mother.

The sun was now setting. The feast prepared by the French residents of Fort Zinna was laid out on long trestle tables. We all sat down higgledy-piggledy, officers and enlisted men, French, British, Italian, and American. Our conversation was in French, which most of the men understood and some spoke. We drank our victory toasts in the wine of André's home region, Champagne. Our cooks and waiters had worked several seasons at Trouville, St. Malô, and the like. And so our celebration feast was a gourmet's delight—broiled spring chicken, fresh asparagus, and new potatoes, all washed down with vintage Barsac. Dessert was apples— the first fresh fruit many of us had had for months—cheese, black bread, and more champagne.

But before joining that memorable celebration, I lay down on my bunk to rest. It was the first time I had really rested since morning, when I undertook the task of fighting my own fear of anarchy by burying the dead, comforting the sick, pacifying the drunks, and keeping the pillaging within bounds. The day had finally hit me. I began shaking violently, uncontrollably. My nervous system, which had lain quiet for so long, had endured too much.

André came over to say something. He looked intently at me, turned, and silently walked away. André was a civilized man.

After returning from the war, GEORGE T. PECK taught history at Lehigh University and then became Vice President and Sales Promotion Manager at the New York clothiers, Peck & Peck. He returned to college teaching in 1970 at Sarah Lawrence College and SUNY Purchase and retired in 1980.

Craig Patrol's view of the Soviet column traveling along the road from Zausswitz. (*Igor Belousovitch*)

Robertson Patrol presents its American flag to Gen. Eisenhower. (*Bill Robertson*)

8. BILL FOX

"The horsemen started galloping toward the Americans."

(Igor Belousovitch)

pril 25, 1945. The dawn was still young, the air cold as six jeeps from E and H Companies rendezvoused with the other two jeeps. The first was the radio jeep from Regiment headquarters, the second from V Corps headquarters.

The scene: the narrow, rickety wooden bridge crossing the Mulde River at Trebsen. The objective: contact the Russian forces approaching from the east through German-held territory.

There were fifty-one men in the patrol. Our eastward advance was limited to five miles beyond the stream. Yet the general feeling among the patrol members was that we were going to keep on until we met the Russians. It was a spirit of eagerness, aggressiveness, and a plain hell-raising desire to make contact. I myself was determined to meet the Russians that day—orders or no orders.

At 4:45 A.M., our patrol left the CP at Trebsen and remained at the bridge. Waiting there in the sharp morning air was unpleasant, but the distant boom of artillery—maybe Russian, maybe German—promised adventure.

Finally, another patrol from the I & R Platoon[1] rattled its way over the old timbers of the Trebsen Bridge and crossed to the east bank. At 5:35, both groups drove east together. Ten minutes later, after parting from the I & R Platoon, our patrol passed through the last outpost and on into the cold dawn fog.

We were theoretically under the command of Second Lt. Thomas P. Howard of Company E. But the patrol was actually directed by Maj. Fred W. Craig, Second Battalion Executive and senior officer present. Capt. George J. Morey, Assistant S-2, had been detailed to represent the Regimental commander, while I had been assigned to cover the story of the Russian-American linkup. I had chosen this patrol as the one most likely to make contact on the Corps front.

The patrol followed a circuitous, sweeping route up and down side roads and main roads through Gornewitz, Denwitz, and Fremdiswalde to Roda. Approaching each town, we slowed down and cautiously reconnoitered before driving in. Small, peasant communities, these towns were for the most part still asleep when our jeeps passed through. Other American patrols had already scouted some of these villages; desultory white flags hung from most of the houses. Here and there, an inquisitive youngster stuck his head out of an upstairs window. Small groups of impassive villagers watched the Americans move silently through the streets. There was no resistance. It was an unreal silence. On that early April morning, war seemed far away in these gray houses and on the lonely, winding roads.

The weather remained cold, the mist persisted. The patrol advanced slowly, carefully, alert to everything around it. After leaving Roda, Maj. Craig decided to go into Wermsdorf. From the distance, we could see a huge red cross glistening from the roof of what appeared to be a big hospital in the town.

We reached Wermsdorf at 9:15 A.M. Driving into the main portion of town, some elements of the patrol went directly to the hospital, while others searched out the area. A number of French, Belgian, Russian, and Polish slave laborers who had been turned into farm workers showed up. Eager to help us, they pointed out German soldiers in hiding. Most of them had simply quit the army.

Patrol members hauled the *bürgermeister* down the center of town. Through an interpreter, Maj. Craig instructed him to tell the population to hang white flags from all houses. All German soldiers were to turn themselves in at the hospital by 3:00 P.M. Any German soldiers seen outside the hospital grounds after that hour would be shot on sight. If any untoward incident occurred, Maj. Craig warned, the *bürgermeister* would be shot and the town leveled by artillery.

Craig Patrol links up amid confusion with Soviet troops near Clanzschwitz. (*Igor Belousovitch*)

Maj. Gen Valdimir Rusakov greets the Craig Patrol on the east bank of the Elbe River near Kreinitz. (*Igor Belousovitch*)

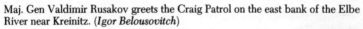

The *bürgermeister* mounted one of the jeeps and repeated these orders to the people who had clustered around in crowds, including freed Allied forced laborers, who looked somewhat puzzled— yet happy—with their new-found liberty. Craig had wisely omitted the fact that he had no artillery to enforce his threat—our handful of men was the entire American army in the area.

We were still within our authorized reconnaissance zone. Wermsdorf was just short of the boundary line set by Regiment. When the patrol had earlier sent a position report, Regiment replied:

Hold patrol in vicinity you are now in. Do not proceed any further. Search that area.

After the patrol reported capturing the hospital in Wermsdorf, Regiment gave the go-ahead to proceed to the north:

Have your patrol proceed to vicinity of (636166) [the town of Deutsch-Luppa-Wendisch]. Search area and report.

At around 11:00 A.M., the patrol pulled out of Wermsdorf and headed up through the central wood which joins the Forsten Wermsdorf and Hubertusburg. Our column went into the forest and stopped at its northern fringe. There we took an entire German sanitary company without trouble. But this caused further delay. By this time, many of us were feeling increasingly eager to meet the Russian forces as soon as possible.

Shortly before noon, we encountered two Russian displaced persons who told us that the Russians had a pontoon bridge across the Elbe at Strehla, that they had patrols in Oschatz during the morning, but that they had withdrawn to Strehla. If the Russians were that far away, it meant that we would have to go beyond our limiting zone to meet them. Yet after having received a clarification of Craig's's report on the capture of the Wermsdorf hospital, Regiment reiterated:

Repeat instructions, you do not proceed beyond new area.

Realizing this, I told Maj. Craig that if his orders precluded such a distant mission, I myself would go on and contact the Russians, providing that he lend me a jeep and his Russian interpreter.

As instructed, the patrol continued on into Deutsch-Luppa-Wendisch. At 1:05 P.M., Craig received another "stay" order. The patrol members were getting more eager to go farther. I repeated my desire to go on.

At three o'clock, our jeeps moved out of Calbitz. All along the route were streams of freed slave laborers and Allied POWs. Some were drunk, others looting. All waved at us and saluted and cheered. They were the flotsam of Europe at that moment—and they were free. Caught in the cataclysm were a number of German civilians who had panicked in the face of defeat. They were on the road in carts, wagons, sulkies, and in anything else which could carry them. They were fleeing—the very old and the very young, the sick and the crippled. They had been caught in the whirlpool of their own nation's collapse, and had now started to join the other wanderers of Europe.

Sometime around four o'clock, the patrol headed for Terpitz. Not far from the Elbe River we stopped on a hilltop to survey the area. We thought we might be able to see the Russian bridgehead from here.

Everyone was suddenly filled with excitement. Through field glasses, we could see several columns of troops moving north over the gentle hill beyond Liebschütz. We questioned a couple of German soldier strays. The troops were German, not Russian, retreating to the north.

We moved east into Clanzschwitz. By then, the roads were very dusty. The air had grown warm, though there was still a chill wind. Moving through the village, the patrol was overtaken by several speeding jeeps. The column halted. The men in the jeeps were from Lt. Kotzebue's patrol. They conveyed the startling news that Kotzebue had made first contact with the Russians in the morning, that he was now on the east bank of the Elbe—not far away.

Craig immediately gave the signal to take off. The jeeps leaped forward, speeding out of town, heading for Leckwitz and the Elbe. After all the jeeps had cleared the last house and the lead vehicle was about 150 yards east of the city limits, the column ground to a halt in a typhoon of dust. Everyone looked to his right with an open-mouthed stare. There, on the tree-lined parallel road leading from Zausswitz, was a column of horsemen moving west. One word came from every amazed mouth: "Russians!"

The horsemen apparently saw the jeeps at the same time, for they wheeled to their right and started galloping toward the Americans. Among the cavalrymen were several soldiers on bicycles and motorcycles. All of us piled out of our jeeps. Time stood still as the first Russian approached.

"I thought the first guy would never get there," one GI later told me. "My eyes were glued to his bike. He seemed to get bigger and bigger as he came slower and slower toward us. He reached a point a few yards away, tumbled off his bike, saluted, grinned, and stuck out his hand. Then they all arrived."

This was the contact. The time was 4:45 P.M. The sun was waning. The day was clear. Everyone grinned. No one could think of anything fancy to say. The Americans said, "*Amerikanski*," the Russians said, "*Russki*." That was it. It was an historic moment, and everyone knew it. But no one could think of any deathless phrases. The only thing that sounded eloquent was the set speech of Pfc. Igor N. Belousovitch of Company E. Born of a Russian family in Shanghai, China, Belousovitch had come along on the patrol as interpreter. To the Russian senior lieutenant who first came up, he said:

> I greet you in the name of the American army and our commanders on this historic occasion. It is a privilege and an honor to be here.

The Russian—equally eloquent—replied:

> This is an historic occasion. It's a moment for which both our armies have been fighting. It's a great honor for me to be here. It is wonderful that we have met in this place. It is a moment which will go down in history.

But those were the only bits of eloquence. For the most part, there was a wholehearted sense of friendship between the two groups. The most elegant thing the majority could do was simply grin and say, "*Tovarisch*." Cameras were out. Pictures were taken. Cigarettes were exchanged. One GI climbed up on one of the Russians' horses and pranced around. Everyone grinned and felt foolish because he couldn't say much. Everyone cursed the language barrier.

The meeting was brief and kaleidoscopic. The Russians, who were troop-size, were attached to the First Guards Zhitomir Cavalry Regiment. They said they were on their way to Dresden and had to hurry. Much had happened, yet nothing had happened.

In little more than three minutes, both groups were on their way. The meeting was over. The time was just past 4:48 P.M.

After making contact, we took off for Strehla, riding furiously in a cloud of dust to join Kotzebue's men at the scene of the original crossing. We found nothing there, backed off, and sped north through Gorzig and across the open stretch of plain to the river bank opposite Kreinitz. On the east shore was another group of Russians. A hand-drawn, crude pontoon ferry stretched across the river.

A few of the Russians immediately started pulling themselves across. When they reached the west side, they drew themselves up, saluted, and leaped ashore. There was more general grinning and handshaking, no one knowing what to say. The command group and a number of the men of our patrol pulled themselves across the swiftly-flowing Elbe to the eastern bank. There, the inevitable Russian cameramen were grinding away.

Coming off the ferry, we swiftly clambered up the sides of the sloping, cobbled bank to the Russian group which clustered around a stocky, firm-faced, small man. We exchanged salutes, at first with a certain reserve. Through Belousovitch, the small man was introduced to us as Maj. Gen. Vladimir Rusakov, commanding general of the Fifty-eighth Guards Infantry Division. The General was cautious at first, asking for identification before he continued.

Gen. Rusakov told us through Belousovitch that his division was part of the First Ukrainian Army, under Col. Gen. Zhadov, and was part of the Army group of Marshal Konyev. They had fought from Stalingrad to the Elbe. The General was, he said, "proud to have my division as the first one to meet the Americans." He was aware of the "historic moment."

But he wanted to know where the rest of the American army was. When was it coming to the Elbe? How much armor was with the infantry? How many Panzers were near? A patrol of a few jeeps just wasn't in the book. His orders, he said, were not to go beyond the Elbe. He was puzzled when we told him that our orders were not to go beyond the Mulde.

Then Gen. Rusakov said something about the Germans running away from the Russians so that they could surrender to the Americans. He was promptly told that the American army had fought hard and well and was not being foolishly soft-hearted with the enemy. That seemed to please him. He hastened to add that he had deep admiration for the American army. Now that we had joined, he said, we would quickly end the war together.

Finally, the exchange of amenities on the river bank was finished. Rusakov said that the members of the Kotzebue Patrol were "being entertained elsewhere." He said the men of our patrol would be taken care of, and then led us officers into a nearby house, where we joined in toasting.

The table was set. Liquor flowed freely. In addition to myself, the officers present were Craig, Morey, Howard, Rusakov, a colonel who was the General's adjutant, and Lt. Col. Alexander Gordeyev, to whom Rusakov pointed with pride and said, "He's my best regimental commander!" Belousovitch interpreted for the group.

We toasted the heads of Russia, Great Britain, and the United States. We toasted the health of every commander and private in both armies. It was "bottoms up" each time—the going got rocky before long. A solemn moment came when we drank a toast to the late President Roosevelt, whom every Russian seemed to know of and for whom they had the greatest respect and affection.

While this military and diplomatic protocol was being taken care of, our radio operator notified Regiment of our linkup. Division proposed sending two planes to the scene. The Russians made preparations for a landing strip. Our patrol leaders sought to arrange a meeting between Col. Charles Adams and Gen. Rusakov. The General said, however, that his instructions were not to go beyond the Elbe; any emissaries would have to come to him.

When the amenities were finished, the Russians offered to take us to an Allied POW camp which had been liberated several days earlier. We accepted, and shortly before dark took off for Ofllg IV-B near Mühlberg; the camp was located just north of Kreinitz. A lieutenant colonel—one of Col. Gordeyev's staff officers—served as our guide.

When the jeeps rolled into the entrance of the camp, it was almost dark, but not too dark to conceal the fact that we were Americans. The reaction was like a tidal wave. The first amazed onlookers exclaimed, "My God! Yanks!" As the jeeps made their way along the streets of the camp, the welcome rose—then roared like thunder. Americans, Britains, French, Yugoslavs, Allied officers and enlisted men of all nations cheered us, screaming and crying their joy. We were just a handful of Americans—no great force.

The camp inmates had already been liberated for several days. Yet the jeeps and American uniforms were symbols of something far closer to them. They stormed our jeeps, taking over the job of driving. As many as could squeeze themselves into a few square inches piled aboard the vehicles and rode around the camp. They were eager just to say hello and shake hands and simply touch these men from the States.

One POW ran alongside a jeep tearing frantically at a Sixty-ninth-Division shoulder patch, trying to get it off the soldier. Finally, he ripped it off with his teeth. "Just a souvenir," he grinned, and kissed it before stuffing it into his pocket. During those minutes, the prisoners were just heartsick guys who had tangible evidence of home after months and years of confinement.

"Where you from?"

"They got me in the Bulge!"

"Bloody bastards took me at Dunkirk!"

"Got me in the Siegfried Line last September!"

"Caught me in Normandy!"

"Shot me down over Bremen!"

"I'm from New York!"

"I'm from London!"

"I'm from San Francisco!"

"I'm from Paris!"

"Parlez-vous français? Je suis belgique!"

These were some of the things they said in wild, confused, enthusiastic outpourings of emotion. But the magnitude of what they left unsaid, of their happiness of at last being free men, was greater than any words could describe. They took us inside the camp and plied us with coffee and talk. More than anything, they wanted to talk, they wanted to ask questions:

"Is it true about Roosevelt's death?"

"Yea, the Jerries treated us better towards the end, even gave us a radio. But the black-souled bastards of SS men were hard and mean."

"Ever stand by helplessly, buddy, and watch another American die in the street after a Nazi rat's shot him? We have. It's not a pleasant sight. We've got no love for those guys."

"Sure, we know you fellas are only a patrol. The rest are back at the Mulde? That's a hell of a place to leave 'em! High command stuff? Well, it won't be long now!"

"Will you autograph this? Okay, I know you're not a celebrity, but you're important as hell to us. Thanks!"

"Have some more coffee. It's not much, but it's all we've got right now."

"Gotta leave? That's too bad. Oh, okay. Sure, sure, we understand. Good luck. So long, boys! Good show, mates! It's almost over now!"

That's what they talked about. That's the way they acted. It was nothing, it was everything. As we left the camp, we were humble men. Though we had done nothing, we were the symbols which those men believed in through long days of prison. We felt proud of our uniforms and our cause.

WILLIAM J. FOX, First Army combat historian, served with the Second Information and Historical Service of V Corps. After the war, he was a news correspondent for United Press International and the *Los Angeles Times*. It was an incredible coincidence that Fox died of natural causes on Elbe Day, April 25, 1986.

1. I & R is an abbreviation for Intelligence and Reconnaissance.

Members of the Craig Patrol and Soviet Soviet soldiers visit the liberated POW camp near Muhlberg, April 25, 1945. (*Alexander Ustinov*)

Ann Stringer interviews Gen. Vladimir Rusakov as Allan Jackson
(with hand in coat pocket) looks on. (*Allan Jackson*)

9. ANN STRINGER

"*Bravo Amerikanski.*"

This was to be my final story from the Front. The series had begun with the dateline *Inside the Juelich Citadel, Germany, Feb. 24, 6:30. P.M.* That story described the Ninth Army's crossing of the Roer River and its dams in the winter of 1944. The Roer Crossing had been the first Allied offensive since the Battle of the Bulge, which had ended the previous month. From there, my datelines had included *Capture of Cologne* (March 5), *On the East Bank of the Rhine at Remagen Bridgehead* (March 10), *With American Troops in Leipzig* (April 11), and *Buchenwald Concentration Camp* (April 21). Yet my final story would prove to be the most historic.

I wasn't even supposed to be at the Elbe—I was in clear violation of orders. My first dateline from the Juelich Citadel had prompted SHAEF to issue a reiteration of its instructions, which were to be brought specifically "to Ann's attention" in the form of an ultimatum. I was to abide by the rule that I go "no farther forward than women's services go." That meant far and away behind the front lines. But I was a United Press newspaperman— not a newspaperwoman. I could write the pants off of any man. So there I was, planning to file the first story of the American linkup with the Soviet Army at the Elbe River. It would have to carry a front-line dateline.

April 26, 1945. Torgau seemed eerily deserted that morning when INS photographer Allan Jackson and I flew over it in separate L-5 Cubs. We knew that American GIs had linked up there with the Russians the previous day. We finally landed in a field of clover on the west bank of the Elbe. We got out of our planes and climbed over a couple of roadblocks to enter the village.

I then saw my first Russian—a young man clad only in a pair of blue shorts and a cap with a red hammer-and-sickle pin. The Elbe River was swarming with Russian soldiers stripped to their shorts, swimming across to greet us. The young man was racing down the street dripping wet. When he saw us, he began shouting, "*Bravo, Amerikanski!*" and "*Bravo*, Comrades!" In great excitement and immediate friendship, the soldier led us to the bank of the river, where we found a couple of battered racing shells. Because all bridges had been demolished by the Germans, we rowed across the Elbe.

As the Russians on the eastern bank saw us coming, they rushed down to the river through the tall, wet grass, and began yelling greetings. Amid shouts of joy and the ebullient shooting of machine guns pointed to the sky, we were met with cries of "*Vive* Roosevelt!" and "*Vive* Stalin!" (The Russians had not been told that President Roosevelt had died only a couple of weeks earlier).

The soldiers helped us drag the racing shell onto the river bank, then all stood rigidly at attention. One by one, they stepped forward, saluted, shook hands, and stepped back into line. Then Lt. Grigori Otenchuku—a veteran of Stalingrad—came forward to make a formal speech on behalf of the Russians.

"A few months ago," he said, "German soldiers were nearly in Stalingrad. Now Russian soldiers are in Berlin, and Russian soldiers are here—all the way across Germany—with their American Allies."

The Russians then insisted that we meet their regimental commander, Maj. Gen. Vladimir Rusakov. We started off. I noticed that almost all of our escort wore at least one brilliantly-colored medal on their greenish tunics.

We were introduced to Maj. Gen. Rusakov, a quiet, stocky man with jet-black hair. He was flanked by his own men as well as by GIs of the Sixty-ninth Infantry Division who had already arrived on the scene. We gave the Russians our autographs. They gave us theirs. The commander invited us to lunch. He told me that I was the first American woman he and his troops had ever seen, and seated me at the luncheon in the place of honor to his right.

Then the toasting began! Toasts to victory, enduring friendship, and everlasting peace. I soon learned that when the Russians toast, it's serious business. We drank toasts in cognac. Then wine. Then schnapps. Then vodka. Then another liquor which I couldn't quite identify, although it tasted much like grain alcohol.

The luncheon itself started with creamed sardines, then highly-seasoned meat patties. Many plates of hard-boiled eggs were passed, as well as plates of raw eggs. The Russians would break one end of the shell of the raw eggs, then suck the yolk and white out.

After the luncheon, we talked with our Russian hosts for about an hour. I had a great story—perhaps the greatest since the D-Day landings—but it was worth nothing unless I could get it filed. I knew I had to head back for Paris, and quickly. I left the Torgau festivities reluctantly, re-entered the racing shell, and asked my pilot if he could fly me to Paris. Quite patiently, he explained that there was *no way* he could fly that L-5 to Paris, but assured me he would fly me as far west as he could.

Carrying my typewriter and the film that Allan had given me to file for him, I climbed aboard the small plane. He headed west. Suddenly, the pilot announced that he had spotted a U.S. C-47 aircraft. We began following it. The C-47 unexplainedly landed in a field, and we landed beside it.

I rushed over to two American airmen and asked if they could fly me to Paris. More than a little amused and puzzled, they asked me what was all the rush. I explained that I had just met the

Russians. It was a *big* story. I *had* to get to Paris to file. With much humor and no little disbelief, both smiled knowingly.

"Oh, yes," one replied. "And I'm Stalin, and he's Roosevelt."

Sensing no point in arguing, I calmly settled on the grass beneath the wing of the C-47. In the shade, I opened my typewriter and started typing. The airmen became puzzled and came by to read over my shoulder. When I looked up to ask their names and hometowns and typed that information into my story, their attitude swiftly changed.

"Hey!" they began shouting. "She met the Russians. She *did* meet the Russians! Let's go!"

We climbed aboard the C-47 and headed for Paris. Landing at the nearest airfield, I still had to hitchhike my way by jeep into Paris. Arriving at the Scribe Hotel—the Press Center for correspondents accredited to U.S. Armies—I went first to the censor's window. There I filed my story, which I had started writing under the wing of the C-47 and completed on the flight to Paris. I filed Allan's film as well. We both thereby gained a clear "beat" on the story of the Elbe linkup. To top it off, Boyd Lewis, the head of United Press at SHAEF, arranged for me to make a broadcast of the exciting linkup.

After the war ended, I had other big stories. Interviews with Austrian Premier Kurt von Schussnigg, Pope Pius XII, and Mussolini's widow. I covered the Nuremburg Trials for United Press. But the story of my meeting in Torgau with the Russians was the biggest one of them all.

ANN STRINGER married fellow reporter Bill Stringer before the war when both were attending the University of Texas. In August 1944, Bill was killed by German tank fire while covering combat for Reuters. Ann shortly thereafter became a United Press correspondent in the European Theater. She, Iris Carpenter of the *Boston Globe*, and Lee Carson of International News Service were dubbed the "Rhine Maidens" by the U.S. military. After the war, Stringer continued to report from Europe before returning to the United States. Today she is a freelance writer in New York City.

American GI embracing Soviet infantryman near Grabow in May 1945. (*AP/Wide World Photos*)

American and Soviet officers dance with Red Army women personnel beneath photos of President Roosevelt and Marshal Stalin near Torgau. FDR's picture is bordered in black in mourning. (*National Archives*)

. . . Because all the bridges were blown, Ann and I crossed the Elbe in a beat-up rowboat that was once apparently a racing shell of some sort. We found a full-blown party in progress on the Russian side of the river. Vodka was flowing, and there was lots of food set up on the tables in an old building. We met a number of American soldiers and low-ranking officers, but no top brass, and—most important to us—no other correspondents. There were lots of Russian soldiers wearing different types of uniforms and carrying a variety of weapons. All of them were very friendly, but the language barrier made conversation difficult. Most talk was carried on in broken German.

I decided that the best way to represent the linkup would be to have a number of American and Russian soldiers stretch their hands towards each other on one of the broken bridges. With the help of a French-speaking Russian soldier who was some sort of official press representative, I rounded up a few Russian and American soldiers to go out on the bridge. I explained what I wanted, and coached them on the action I planned for my photograph ('Don't look at the camera!'). I made several shots of the action, trying for angles of faces that did not look directly into the lens.

Two days later—on April 28—my photo hit the front page of the major London newspapers. It was, the *News Chronicle* reported, 'a picture the world will never forget.' That same day, it was on the front page of the *New York Times* and many other American newspapers. Through the years, my picture of the American and Russian soldiers shaking hands at Torgau has been called the second best-known photograph of World War II. Only Joe Rosenthal's flag-raising photo on Iwo Jima is better known.

—ALLAN JACKSON

Allan Jackson's famous picture of American and Soviet soldiers
shaking hands across a broken bridge at Torgau.

10. ANDY ROONEY

"Trading Day Along the Elbe."
from Stars and Stripes, April 28, 1945

With Konyev's Ukrainian Army, April 26 (Delayed)—There was a mad scene of jubilant celebration on the east and west banks of the Elbe at Torgau today, as infantrymen of Lt. Gen. Courtney H. Hodges' First U.S. Army swapped K rations for vodka with soldiers of Marshal Konyev's First Ukrainian Army and congratulated each other, despite the language barrier, on the linkup, which means the defeat of the German Army as a fighting unit.

Men of the 69th Inf. Div. sat on the banks of the Elbe in warm sunshine today, with no enemy in front of them, and drank wine, cognac and vodka while they watched their new Russian friends and listened to them as they played accordions and sang Russian songs.

Russian soldiers, strong and young looking, built a little heavier and shorter than most Americans, inspected American equipment and Americans took the chance to fire the Russian automatic rifle. When the day was over many a U.S. soldier walked back to his jeep in Russian boots while the Russian soldier he traded with fought with the straps on his newly acquired GI shoes.

If today was not an extraordinary day in the lives of most Russians along the Elbe at Torgau, then Russian soldiers are the most carefree bunch of screwballs that ever came together in an Army. They would be best described as exactly like Americans only twice as much.

If you know what a German soldier is like, the Russian soldier seems to be his direct opposite. It is impossible to imagine a regimented, goose-stepping Russian. They sing and laugh and cut patterns with their tommy-guns up against brick walls.

The road into Torgau was a strange scene. Russian laborers who have been working German farms were streaming down the highway into Torgau to contact their army which at last had come to liberate them. Across the road, going in the other direction, there was a column of sullen, tired, frightened people—Germans fleeing from the Russian Army.

When the caravans reached the river edge where Russian troops were mingling with Americans, the Russian soldiers went to talk and sing and make love with young Russian girls that had come in on wagons. They formed in groups of twenty around accordions and sang Russian songs, all of which sounded like the Volga Boat song to most Americans.

ANDREW A. ROONEY is a well-known newspaper columnist and television commentator. During World War II, he was a war correspondent for *Stars and Stripes.*

(*National Archives*)

GIs singing to the accompaniment of a Soviet accordion player at Torgau.

11. HAROLD DENNY

"These Russkys are pretty good boys."
      from the New York Times, *April 28, 1945*

A t a Red Army outpost, on the Elbe, April 27—The United States and Russian armies have met on the Elbe. The Western and Eastern fronts are at last linked up, and Germany is cut in two . . .

On the American side, the honor of making this historic junction goes to Gen. Courtney H. Hodges's United States First Army, which forced the Normandy beaches last June and has advanced seven hundred miles through France, Belgium, and Germany to this spot. On the Russian side, it goes to Marshal Ivan S. Konyev's First Ukrainian Army, which has fought its way 1,400 miles from Stalingrad in one of the greatest marches against bitter opposition in all history . . .

The spirit in which the American and Russian troops and their local commanders met was worthy of the great occasion. The Russians received us with open-handed hospitality, and our men have responded in kind. From the moment the first American patrol was taken into a Russian forward command post, it has been almost a continuous party.

There was handshaking and backslapping among the troops who made the first contacts. The Russians laid out front-line banquets of food and vodka, and the Americans produced brandy and champagne "liberated" from German Army stores, and there were toasts and songs and expressions of hope for the future in which America, Russia, and Britain would stand together for enduring peace.

There is something kindred in the warm-hearted, uninhibited cordiality of the Russians, such as we have met these past three days, and the hearty friendliness of the average GI. Our soldiers and the Russians have got along beautifully thus far. The American attitude in the frontline might be summed up in the remark of one jeep driver: "These Russkys are pretty good boys."

The enthusiastic cordiality of the Russian and American dough-boys extended on up through the meetings of Col. Charles M. Adams, commander of the 273rd Regiment and his Russian counterpart, between Gen. Reinhardt and the Soviet division commander, and at a meeting today of Gen. Huebner and the Soviet corps commander . . .

We found a town badly battered, some of its buildings still burning, but no Russian troops. We circled the town cautiously and then entered it past a slave labor camp whose inmates waved at us.

We drove through a square past a statue of Frederick the Great and stopped in another large square. Then someone shouted, and we saw walking almost majestically from the archway of a building a tall young Russian who turned out to be Lt. Ivan Feodorovich Kuzminski of Kirovograd, commanding the outpost in the city. His men followed him. The American soldiers accompanying us made a rush for them, and in seconds the Russians and Americans were clasping hands, exchanging names, and trying to express mutual gratification.

A score of Russian soldiers strolled up and were friends with the Americans instantly. They produced bottles of cognac and cham-pagne "liberated" from German Army stores and rolled out a barrel of German beer and treated the Americans. Several Russian soldiers had accordions, and they and our GIs joined in a song-fest—which was a greater social than a musical success, inasmuch as the Americans sang "Swanee River" while the Russians rendered "If There Should Be War Tomorrow," a Soviet patriotic ballad.

A Red Army "Wac" walked down the street to join us—Sgt. Anna Konstantinovna Eugenia of Kharkov—and sang another Russian patriotic song of Soviet greetings to the English and American peoples.

Late in the afternoon, Gen. Reinhardt arrived and was met by the Russian commander with his staff all turned out smartly. Again there were toasts. The Russian cavalry showed its skill, and there were mutual congratulations on our two armies' military successes.

Thus passed auspiciously the first twenty-four hours of the linkup of our two great victorious forces.

12. BEN CASMERE

"We just came over the river to greet your army."

W hen I met the Russians, I was a machine gun corporal with the 261st Field Artillery Battalion, U.S. Ninth Army. On April 24, we moved east from Siedengreben to Gross Ellingen—just west of the Elbe River. Our artillery did little firing from this position, since we had orders not to fire on any target which had not been definitely identified as armed enemy forces.

Rumors were rampant that the Russians were close. When large numbers of German soldiers began crossing the Elbe in our direction, we knew the Russians were not far behind. Odds ran high that the war was coming to an end.

By the morning of May 3, the 406th Infantry, 102nd Division, had dug in on the west bank of the Elbe near Sandau. Expecting the Russians, the 102nd had erected a large sign facing the east bank. It was in Russian, but written in English letters. The grammar wasn't the best, but the feeling was there. The way the Russians read it was something like:

CHEERS TO THE RUSHAN ARMY!
We're all hear, Josef
FROM U.S.—406th INFANTRY
102 DIVISION—9th ARMY
AMERICAN ARMY

On the morning of May 3, I went to the 406th Infantry's dug-in position with my buddy Pfc. Bruce Waugh and "Poochie," a little dog I'd adopted a couple of weeks earlier. Bruce and I knew something was going to happen that day because we hadn't seen any German soldiers on the west bank. The preceding week, they'd been there every single day.

The 406th spotted troop movements on the other shore, and ordered us to take firing positions. It was a nice, clear morning—good visibility.

Suddenly, someone on the opposite side raised a red and white flag. I shouted, "God Almighty! It's a Polish flag!" as I ran to the shoreline waving my arms in friendship. Right then and there, I assured my buddy Bruce that everything was O.K.

We decided to cross the river to greet the soldiers on the other side. Bruce, Poochie, and I got into one of the rowboats the Germans had abandoned.

On the east bank, we met soldiers of the First Ukrainian Army with elements of a large Polish division. We celebrated with kissing, hugging, and backslapping. I never kissed so many men in my life. It was a thrilling, happy moment. The war was still going on. We were at the front lines. But we knew peace was near. We enjoyed meeting each other with all our hearts and souls.

Bruce and I had brought along two packages of K rations and a pack of cigarettes each. We passed these around, sharing with the Russian and Polish troops. We didn't have enough cigarettes to go around, so everyone who already had one split it and passed the halves to others who wanted to smoke. We split the K rations the same way.

The Russians and Poles really liked our steel helmets and combat boots. Even though I'd grown up in a Polish-speaking family back in the States, I was having a rough time translating. I wasn't acquainted with many of the words. Our friends mainly wanted to know where we came from and what news we had of the war. Some said they had relatives in America.

A high-ranking Russian officer then appeared. He talked loudly, quickly to Bruce and me until I replied, *"Niet poyia mia po rusku"* ("I don't speak Russian") and *"Prozie po polskie mowsjie"* ("Please speak Polish"). The officer calmed down, realizing we needed an interpreter. Two Polish soldiers came up to us and translated the officer's question: "Are you representing your officers for a meeting?"

"No," I replied. "We just came over the river to greet your army. We will relay your message."

The officer said, "You must return to your side of the river. We wouldn't want you to be injured here by the enemy."

Just then, we heard rifle and machine gun fire a short distance away.

"There," he said. "See what I mean?"

I answered, "We do now."

We exchanged salutes. The officer smiled and wished us well.

When it was time to leave, a Russian soldier reached over and handed me a small coin as a gift in exchange for what we had brought to share. Bruce, Poochie, and I were very happy when we jumped back into the rowboat and returned to the west bank.

Later that day, two Russian soldiers crossed the river and met one of our officers, Maj. Raymond T. Chapman. Another brief celebration took place. We all began thinking of home.

It's been more than forty years now, but I've never forgotten the moment of peace and friendship that this American corporal had with the Russians on that clear, sunny day in May. In April of 1986, a group of Russian Elbe veterans visited Detroit. Boy! Oh Boy! Did it ever bring back memories.

I gave a short speech at a reception for them, telling everyone about my linkup in 1945. Then I gave each of them a Susan B. Anthony silver dollar in remembrance of the small coin the Russian soldier gave me at the Elbe. One of the Russians didn't quite understand what I was doing. With a puzzled look, he asked me through an interpreter, "What is this coin? Why? What for?"

The interpreter explained. A broad smile spread across the Russian's face. He kissed me on both cheeks. We laughed and hugged the same way as at the linkup. The "Spirit of the Elbe" was there in Detroit that night, just as it had been with us when Bruce and I met the Russians in the last days of the war.

BERNARD F. ("BEN") CASMERE (KAZMIERSKI) is a retired real estate broker.

Waugh and Casmere with Polish soldiers on the east bank of the Elbe. (*Ben Casmere*)

An American, Soviet, and British soldier share a pack of cigarettes on the east bank of the Elbe. (*Signal Corps Photo*)

Women paramedics of the Soviet Fifty-eight Guards Division serve food at the celebrations near Torgau. (*National Archives*)

Iris Carpenter of the *Boston Globe* interviewing Soviet officers at Torgau, April 26, 1945. (*Natl. Archives*)

Barney Oldfield makes General Dwight D. Eisenhower, an honorary member of the post war Press Club of Berlin. (*U.S. Army Signal Corps Photo*)

Ann Stringer (fourth from left) joins with Soviet hosts in a vodka toast to victory near Torgau. (*Source: Ann Stringer*)

13. Cecil Ellzey

"For two hours, I was treated like a king."

Those of us in the U.S. Eighth Infantry Division knew that American troops had already linked up with the Russians along the Elbe River some two hundred miles south of our position. On April 29, we were preparing to jump across the Elbe with the Eighty-second Airborne on our right and the Sixth British Airborne on our left. Both were part of Gen. Matt Ridgway's XVIII Corps.

I was a liaison pilot and Assistant Division Air Officer with the Eighth Infantry. On the afternoon of April 29, I let Gen. Ridgway have two piloted planes to fly over to Gen. Montgomery's headquarters to find out what the British commander planned to do. Gen. Ridgway returned, thanked me for the planes, and told me that in the morning we would jump off for the Baltic Sea to meet the Russians.

Late in the afternoon of the following day, forward elements of our forces reached Schwerin, Germany. Higher headquarters halted our drive at that point. We in the Air Section occupied an abandoned airfield near Schwerin. Life got to be interesting here. We lived in the tower, and had 4,000-foot runways for our Piper Cubs (L-4s). German soldiers were surrendering by the tens of thousands. The plight of these supposed Supermen was a sad one indeed. We did not realize that so many of them were still alive. Yes, I had had experiences to last me a lifetime. I was ready to return home.

Early in the afternoon of May 3 I received a call from Gen. James A. Pickering, Commanding General of the Eighth Infantry Division Artillery. He had a mission for me. This was not too unusual. He had given me missions before, some not very desirable. Gen. Pickering assigned me a news correspondent, who was with either the *New York Daily Times* or the *New York Daily Sun.*

Division gave me clearance to locate forward elements of the Red Army and help the reporter get a story.

The correspondent arrived shortly thereafter, and we took off to the north in my L-4. The L-4 was a special plane. It provided commanders not only with adjustment of forward observation fire, but also with the kind of current reconnaissance information never before available to ground commanders. The reporter told me he wanted a story for his New York paper, and promised me a copy—which I never received.

Approximately twenty minutes from the airfield—after passing over our troops—I observed a long convoy of Russian vehicles on the tree-lined road east of Warin. I purposely flew low so that the American markings could be seen, being very cautious not to fly near or over their convoy as I searched for a field on which to land. During the war I had had some uncomfortable flights over our armor. I learned not to fly over any military convoy.

I found a large open field alongside the convoy and put the plane down. We did not roll any distance because the wheat was so tall. We came to a quick stop. Assuming that the correspondent spoke Russian, I opened the door. A Russian soldier stood there holding an automatic weapon on us. I waited for the reporter to say something. With my hands over my head, I finally realized that he was so scared he could not speak.

I quickly made frantic noises, saying *"Amerikanski"* several times over. Quite likely, I made other sounds in an attempt to convince the Russian to lower the barrel of his weapon. After these uncomfortable moments, the Russians welcomed us with bear hugs and escorted us to what evidently was their kitchen vehicle, which offered drinks served by female personnel.

The Russians furnished transportation into Warin for the correspondent, who pointed to his destination on a map. I stayed with the troops, spending most of the time making toasts in sign language. We laughed together, exchanged notes and gifts. The Russians gave me a lady's fourteen-carat gold watch, which has all the hallmarks inside the outer case; to this day, my wife wears the watch on a neck chain for special occasions.

I gave the Russians my Zippo lighter and part of a pack of cigarettes. For two hours, I was treated like a king. The Russians liked their drinks and wanted me to enjoy them too, which was no problem as far as I was concerned. My hosts were in high spirits and very hospitable. They impressed me to no end.

When the reporter returned, he thought I may have had too much to drink. But I was ready to fly the aircraft back to Schwerin. I explained to the Russians that some vehicle was needed to knock down the wheat for a clear runway. They obliged. Not more than one hundred feet in front of the plane their truck fell into a huge shell hole. The incident made me realize that my thinking was not dull. It actually helped make me more alert. The Russians cleared a long runway, for which I was grateful.

The correspondent and I returned without incident to the airfield at Schwerin. When we landed, he hurriedly left the plane— he thought the Russians had given me too much to drink.

My feelings about my meeting with the Russians more than forty years ago remain unchanged. I know that there is a basic difference in our governments. But as a people, we do not differ to any large degree. And I believe that the cause of that difference is not insurmountable. The Russians do not want war any more than we do, for they know the devastation war would bring.

CAPT. CECIL C. ELLZEY of Tylertown, Mississippi, returned from the war to serve with distinction in the Louisiana National Guard. Ellzey subsequently became administrator of the Bogalusa Community Medical Center in Bogalusa, Louisiana. He retired in 1985.

A woman wearing a fox stole stands bewildered in front of a German train station. (*Ullstein Bilderdienst*)

A homeless German family in 1945. The sign around the girl's neck reads,
"Schlesinger. We're looking for work and shelter." (*Ullstein Bilderdienst*)

14. JEFF BOEHM

"If they are Americans, they should not be behind barbed wire!"

I was a radio operator and gunner serving with the 440th Bomb Squadron, 319th Bomb Group of the U.S. Army Air Force. On January 22, 1944, our B-26 was shot down over Italy. The pilot and navigator tried to take the stricken plane back to our base, but they died when it crashed into a mountain side and blew up. Two of the gunners opened their parachutes too soon; both men were whipped into the flames of the aircraft, burned, and dropped like stones 10,000 feet. The co-pilot and I were captured when we parachuted to earth. We were moved by truck and freight trains up into Germany.

My memories of being an American POW liberated by Russian troops in Nazi Germany are as clear as if it all had taken place yesterday. I remember when the Germans marched us out of *Kriegsgefangenen Lager III* in Heydekrug in July of 1944. They were taking us to another POW camp because the Red Army was getting too close. About 2,500 of us were marched out of the Heydekrug compound that day. When we came to the main road, we found it filled with refugees, pushing and pulling different kinds of wheeled vehicles. In the place of horses, old men and women had harnessed themselves to wagons. Little kids were pulling express wagons, all piled high with the bundles of those things refugees take from their abandoned homes because they think they can carry them.

The city of my fathers, how can I yet find it?
Following the swarms of bombers
I come home.
Where is it then? Over there, amid

99

Mountains of rising smoke,
There amid The flames.

The city of my fathers, how will it welcome me?
The bombers precede me, the deadly swarms
Announce my homecoming. Conflagrations
Precede the son's return.
                                            —BERTOLT BRECHT

They moved slowly, the road filled from side to side. Occasionally, I could see a child in hiking shorts with a back pack, but most of the children—like the old people—were dressed poorly. There wasn't a sound, except for a squeaky wheel or the shuffle of feet. Hours went by before we could find a break in the slowly moving column.

When we finally got to the train, we heard from others that our guards had to threaten oncoming refugees with fixed bayonets to keep us all together. We were jammed into forty-and-eight boxcars (built to carry forty soldiers or eight horses). As usual, the Germans put sixty-five of us in each car. Our group filled at least one train. Each of us had been issued about a quarter loaf of army bread. There'd be water stops in the morning and afternoon.

I can still remember a young German woman sitting on a box near our car. She is holding a baby and a cup of soup. Tears are running down her gaunt face as she tries to feed the soup to the baby, as the soup runs down the baby's dress. There is no one else near her, no reason for her not to nurse the child. But she herself hasn't had enough to eat, and so no longer has milk for the baby.

After several days of often-interrupted travel, we were loaded into the hold of a steamer. Our guards packed us in; even if all of us could have remained standing, there still wouldn't have been enough room. We literally sweated our urine out. Maybe once a day, the guards lifted the hatch cover of our hold and lowered a bucket of water. The prisoners within reach fought over it. A few got a gulp, but it looked as if most of it was spilled in the shoving.

We traveled on the steamer for two or three days, then were unloaded for another train. This time, we were handcuffed in fours. One of the guards told us that they were cuffing us because of a report that the Allies were handcuffing German POWs. We were then loaded into boxcars which were divided in half by a wire screen. On the other side of the screen were six guards with a machine gun.

After a while, we and the guards relaxed and swapped cigarettes. One of the prisoners had a key like that used to open a sardine can; we used it to unlock our cuffs. It was so hot in there, with nothing to drink. At about noon, the train stopped. We re-locked our cuffs, and tumbled out of the car to find a new outfit ready to take charge from there.

We are met by a large contingent of young soldiers armed with fixed bayonets. A tough-looking colonel screams at us. (We later learn that his wife and kids had been killed in the Dresden bombing.) The soldiers have several German shepherds on leashes. The boys lead us down a road in columns of four and five. Soon they order us to run. Just ahead of us several of our guys fall; some are so dehydrated they are sweating blood. One of them can't get up, and the prisoner handcuffed to him can't pull him up. The Colonel runs up and orders the dogs turned loose. They attack the guy on the ground, who tries to roll himself up in a ball.

The Colonel notices that one guard has refused to bayonet the fallen POW. He screams an order at him. The young soldier snaps to attention—eyes straight ahead—and holds it. The Colonel orders the other guards to take him away. We help carry the bloody POW to the camp. The British medics count seventy-six dog bites and bayonet wounds on him. He survives. Yet we doubt if the young German soldier who disobeyed orders is still alive.

The last days of the war. We were in *Stalag Luft I* near Barth, a fishing and farming community on the Baltic Sea. Hungry days and nights, especially for those in their twenties. Some lost fifty pounds in six weeks. One or two of them regularly collapsed during roll call.

It would have been much worse if the Germans had made us work, but because we were all officers (most non-commissioned) and Geneva Convention rules exempted us from work, they didn't require it. They did, however, require all Red Army POWs in the camp—regardless of rank—to do the dirty and hard work around the four compounds, always accompanied by a squad of armed guards.

Nearly all the 2,500 men in our compound had been in bomber crews except for a small group of fighter pilots who out-ranked the rest of us. Most of us were sergeants who had come from camps like *Stalag III* at Heydekrug and *Stalag IV* at Kiefheyde. Col. F.S. ("Gabby") Gabreski, the "famous ace," was the commander of our compound.

On the afternoon of April 29, there was an earth-shaking explosion just outside the compound. And two more! We hit the dirt. Huge brown clouds of dust and debris bloomed over barracks tops. "They're getting ready to leave!" And that's just what it was. The Germans were blowing up power and light sources and junctions, utilities, not only supplying the camp, but also nearby Barth. That evening, we crowded around the loudspeakers hoping for news of what was happening in the outside world. The German reports had been almost as accurate as the BBC news we got from our hidden receivers. The Germans had scored two news beats on BBC, reporting the opening of the Second Front twenty-four hours ahead of the Allies, and breaking the news of President Roosevelt's death.

The ranks of insomniacs had been increasing. By ten o'clock that night, the barracks hall would be filled on both sides with sitting or sprawling Kriegies, their cigarettes winking like little stars. They were sure we'd be bombed at night, and thought the hall was the safest place to sit it out. But it was still too early for the night watch. The sunset was just beginning to fade. Four guys in Room 12 were cooking a cat they had caught. Others stood around, watching. "Just as good as rabbit," one said.

The Chief stood in the doorway. "I'm not hungry," he said. The Chief was forty-six then, slightly over five feet tall, lean and hard. A naturalized American, he spoke fluent Russian, having been born in Russia and educated in Germany from age eight. He had served in the German Army on both the Western and Eastern fronts in World War I before immigrating to the States. A Jew, he had been passing himself off as a Navajo Indian since his capture by Hungarians. As a tail-gunner on our B-24s, he had been shot down on his ninety-ninth mission near Budapest and was nearly lynched by peasants before one of their leaders decided that he was an Indian. Having seen Indians in American Western films, they considered them their peers in horsemanship, the Chief said.

We went outside.

"You think we'll get out of this alive?" I asked him.

"It won't be long now," the Chief replied. "You guys worrying about what's going to happen to you need to stop and think about what's going on beyond that wire. Red Army soldiers, most of them living on little hunks of bread and cheese, and maybe a little soup, are winning the war while you're sitting on your asses moping. Lots of them are women, and they're fighting and dying in action right now."

I knew he was right. We had just received our own BBC reports that the Russians had taken Stettin, seventy miles east of us. They were coming our way. I looked across our compound through the barbed wire to the west. Through those trees was the Baltic. Across the seas was home. The sunset on the water faded. The Chief and I went inside.

The shutters were closed in our room. Two men were tinkering with the lamp—a wick cut from a GI belt in a can of margarine. Most of the marge wasn't good enough to eat anyway, so it made sense to get some light out of it. Sacked out, we talked, argued, described how Mom made turkey stuffing or the best way to use Klim, the powdered milk we got from the Red Cross. It was about ten o'clock when somebody yelled, "The Jerries are gone! The lights in the towers ain't movin'!" We all hit the floor together. "They're leavin' us here!" Shutters were opened cautiously as somebody put out the marge. Those searchlights on the guard towers which had always been moving over the compound before were still lit. There must have been an emergency generator for them. But they were motionless.

Hardly anyone slept that night. At dawn, we were roaming the compound. The barracks doors had been padlocked, so we went out through the windows or the carefully hidden trap doors we had cut in our floors. No guards. No dogs. Everything seemed peaceful.

The next day, the barracks were deserted by all but a few who were washing clothes or making Victory Cakes, some of which were two feet square with five layers. Baked in tin pans made from several flattened Klim cans, with toothpowder (it contained some soda) to make them rise, they were made from ground bread and C-ration crackers, plus raisins and prunes, chocolate D-bars and other sweets hoarded over many months.

It was dusk when we saw the first flare, far off over the trees to the west. Like a bright red ball, it floated in a slow, flat curve and was gone! A few seconds later, three more—one red, two blue—rose in the same trajectory.

"Infantry flares," the Chief said. "Red Army!"

The loudspeaker system had been repaired during the day, and a "Hit Parade" was coming over it. At about ten o'clock that night, an announcer broke in on "Don't Fence Me In" with a news bulletin:

We've made contact with the Russians! BBC reports the Red Army has taken Berlin. Hitler is dead!

The news spread like a flash fire. We rushed from the rooms into the hall, surged against the front doors, crashed through and streamed out into the compound. All the other barracks were popping open. The 2,500 of us were yelling, screaming, whistling, waving, leaping on one another, laughing like maniacs, howling at the sky. When there was a lull in our compound, we heard great roaring waves of sound from the other three. It went on and on. We couldn't stop until we lost our voices. A long time later, when the shouting had almost subsided, you could hear single voices from other compounds, "Uncle Joe! Yay! Uncle Joe!"

At eight o'clock on the morning of May 1, Gabreski called us out for assembly. We were no longer prisoners, he said, "but we're still soldiers, and this is now an army camp." He said we'd be moving for home as soon as possible. Home! And, he said, the Russians had requested that we wear black armbands in mourning for President Roosevelt. Those of us who couldn't find black cloth or paper marked the band on our sleeve with a pencil. At roll call, we were dismissed after the count, but not a man moved. We stood at attention for a full minute in memory of FDR.

On the afternoon of that second day, we tore down the barbed wire. All around the compound, we tore into that wire with whatever we could improvise as tools from the wood and metal of our barracks. Those who had overthrown the western fence stormed across the road and wrecked a Nazi storage barracks, smashing windows and doors, ramming it with four-by-fours from the guard towers until it rocked off its foundation and collapsed.

That night visitors came to our room. They were eleven of the former Red Army prisoners who had been quartered in a small adjacent compound. The Germans had used them in our compound about twice a week, bringing them in under heavy guard with a tank wagon to bail out the pit under the latrine. A few of us had managed to toss cigarettes to them occasionally when the guards weren't looking.

The Chief had sometimes managed a brief conversation with one of them, a sergeant who always wore a Cossack cap. He was a fighter pilot, the Chief said, who had once tossed a handful of fresh onions to him. The wonderful smell of those onions in our room's potato stew almost drove the other guys in our barracks around the bend!

Well, our visitors are led by the guy in the Cossack cap, and he and the Chief are having a noisy reunion, shouting in Russian back and forth as the rest of us look on. Some of us suddenly realize that we are the hosts, and make Spam and tuna sandwiches and coffee for our guests. There's handshaking all around. Everybody's grinning. Eleven Russians and the twenty-four of us are all crowded in a room about fifteen by twenty-four feet, narrowed by the triple-decker bunks on each side. But we can sit on the table and benches, and the shelf under the windows. We and our guests are used to cramped quarters.

After a while, the Chief begins to translate what the Russians told him. "Ninety-eight of the Russian POWs were murdered by the Germans just before they left," he says. "They were taken from their barracks in the afternoon and marched to a French concentration camp about three miles away. These eleven men escaped into the woods when they guessed there was trouble ahead. But they followed along. They saw the rest of their comrades forced to dig a deep trench at gun point, then lined up in front of it and mowed down by machine gun fire."

When the Russian in the Cossack cap had first arrived at our compound, he told our brass he was amazed that the barbed wire fence was still standing. "Who are these men behind the wire?" he asked, "And who are the men in the guard towers?"

"These are our own men," he was informed. "We are guarding them so they won't get out and take off where we wouldn't be able to find them."

"If they are Americans," the Russian said, "they are liberated, and they should not be behind barbed wire! They are free men. You should open the gates and let them enjoy their freedom!" The Cossack began shouting, "They should be in the town celebrating their freedom and the great victory with us, eating good food, sleeping in clean beds, instead of being in these stinking barracks!"

Red Army troops moved in to relieve the Cossack sergeant. For days, I rambled about with the Chief, glad to be able to question the Russian soldiers. We talked with a boy of twelve—a war orphan—who said, "The army is my mother and father." We talked with a physician who had been working night and day to save the few survivors of a nearby concentration camp.

By May 4, the Red Army had repaired all utilities for our camp and for Barth. It had cleared the airfield of mines and tested it for takeoffs and landings. The Russians had set up a new administration in Barth, and had notified Allied HQ in London that we were liberated and that the airfield was ready for use. They had also rounded up cows and pigs—fresh meat—for us.

Most of us left the camp on May 13, when in a very impressive show of air power swarms of B-17s shuttled us out of Barth on the first leg of our return from the war.

Yes, my memories of our liberation are as clear as if it happened only yesterday. Today—in the Soviet Union, all over Europe, in Japan, and here in the United States—the graves of millions of soldiers and non-combatants killed in World War II receive their tribute of flowers, of tears, and of memories from those who survived. And there are tears for other millions, millions of mothers, fathers, daughters and sons who became piles of shoes, clothes, teeth, hair, lard, lampshades, and ashes. For them, there are no graves.

I yet see faces, so many faces, which have not grown old in my mind over the years. The desperate faces of the countless refugees choking the dusty country roads of a devastated Germany. The drawn face of that weeping mother with no milk for her child. The faces of snarling guard dogs and of a young German soldier who died rather than violate his conscience. The face of the Chief, and Gabreski, and the Russian sergeant in the Cossack cap. And yes, those faces of joy and hope when Russian soldiers liberated our American POW camp not so long ago, when we and the Russians had our own special linkup.

GODFREY E. ("JEFF") BOEHM returned from the war to pursue a career as a labor reporter. He retired in 1983.

Jeff and wife Marjorie Boehm on April 25, 1985, in Torgau. (*Photo courtesy Jeff Boehm*)

II: From Stalingrad

Soviets wave farewell to U.S. soldiers crossing back to the west bank of the Elbe.

to the Elbe

Edited by Semyon Krasilshchik

(*Novosti Press*)

Generals Reinhardt and Rusakov lead a procession of Soviet and American
soldiers from the east bank of the Elbe for celebration held in the nearby village
of Werdau, April 27, 1945. (*National Archives*)

15. ALEXEI ZHADOV

"May this meeting be a guarantee of a stable and lasting peace on our planet!"

The main force of the Fifth Guards Army, which I commanded, was advancing rapidly—thirty to forty kilometers a day. Early on April 23, our advance units—and later that day our main force—reached the Elbe in the vicinity of Elster, Prettin, Torgau, and Riesa. None of the advance units which had arrived at the Elbe on April 23 reported the presence of any U.S. troops in the area. It was only on April 25 that the historic linkup took place, to our soldiers' great joy and happiness.

How did it happen?

On April 25 at 1:30 P.M., the men of the Sixth Company of the 175th Guards Infantry Regiment, Fifty-eighth Guards Division, sighted a group of soldiers advancing from the west near Strehla. The Company was commanded by Senior Lt. Grigori Goloborodko, formerly a machine fitter from Poltava. Naturally, our men were on the alert, but they had enough combat experience to realize that the group approaching was by no means the enemy they'd been fighting so long. Nevertheless, Goloborodko's men were combat-ready as they moved forward to meet the unknown detachment. It turned out to be a reconnaissance patrol of the Sixty-ninth Division, U.S. First Army, led by Lt. Albert Kotzebue, a former student from Texas. He was accompanied by his sergeants and men, including Joseph Polowsky.

About an hour later, men of the Second Battalion, 173rd Guards Infantry Regiment of the Fifty-eighth Guards Division, sighted a man in military uniform signaling from the belfry of a church in the city of Torgau. Lt. Alexander Silvashko tried signaling back to him in German, but the man didn't seem to understand. Our soldiers fired into the air several times, and suddenly heard the familiar response, "Moscow-America!" The man in the belfry was an

111

American. Indeed, he turned out to be a soldier with the Sixty-
ninth Infantry Division. A U.S. officer soon came out to meet the
Soviet soldiers. He said he and his men were a reconnaissance
patrol of the Sixty-ninth Infantry Division, U.S. First Army, and
invited the Soviet officer to visit his battalion's HQ located about
fifteen kilometers away.

We later learned that the patrol was commanded by Second Lt.
William Robertson.

At 11:30 P.M., Soviet representatives arrived at the headquarters
of the U.S. Sixty-ninth Division, forty kilometers west of the
Elbe.They included Maj. Anafim Larionov, deputy commander of
the 173rd Guards Infantry Regiment; Capt. Vasili Nyeda, commander of the Second Infantry Battalion of the same regiment; Lt.
Silvashko; and Sergeant Nikolai Andreyev.

The meetings of Soviet and American officers and men vividly
expressed their wartime friendship, interest in each other, and
shared joy over the imminent and total defeat of Nazi Germany.
Both the officers and men of the Allied armies embraced each
other with emotion, then exchanged mementoes. Within minutes,
many of our men had buttons removed from their tunics and coats.
The five-pointed red stars were gone from their caps. The U.S.
soldiers were also quite interested in our Guards insignia and our
medals bearing the inscription "For the Defense of Stalingrad."
Army capes were spread over the ground and the soldiers covered
them with cans of food, bread, vodka, and whiskey. The men
drank to their linkup, to victory, to peace and friendship. There
were language problems, of course, but the soldiers showed great
presence of mind and seemed quite capable of understanding each
other. Breaking into smaller groups, they had friendly discussions,
told each other about their own combat experiences, showed
photos of their families, posed for pictures, and traded autographs.

On the evening of April 25, staff officers of the Fifty-eighth
Guards Division made contact with the HQ of the U.S. Sixty-ninth
Division. The following day, a regimental commander of the Sixty-
ninth and the commander of our 173rd Guards Regiment met. An
archival document describes that meeting as follows:

> The meeting took place at 11:00 A.M. on a bridge crossing
> the Elbe near Torgau. Other officers from both sides were
> present. Comrade Rogov and the U.S. regimental com-

mander made brief remarks. Both emphasized the need to establish a close friendship between the two nations and armies, and join together in hastening the final defeat of Nazi Germany.

Later that day, Maj. Gen. Vladimir Rusakov, Commander of the Fifty-eighth Guards Division, met with Maj. Gen. Emil Reinhardt, Commander of the U.S. Sixty-ninth Division. About seventy American, British, French, and Soviet news correspondents and several cameramen were also at the meeting.

At six o'clock on the evening of April 26, our troops contacted Allied forces in the zone occupied by the 118th Infantry Division on the west bank of the Elbe. The first Soviet officers to meet the Americans were Capt. Ushakov, commander of the First Company, 527th Infantry Regiment, and Lt. Kondrashov, platoon commander. A group of American soldiers led by Lt. H.W. Shank drove up in a jeep to our detachment's position. They were met by our men, and later by officers Ushakov and Kondrashov. The Americans were a reconnaissance patrol of the U.S. 104th Infantry Division, commanded by Maj. Gen. Terry Allen. The soldiers of the two Allied armies first saluted each other, then shook hands.

And so two weeks before the end of the war in Europe, the soldiers of the Soviet Fifth Guards Army had linked up with the troops of the U.S. First Army, commanded by Gen. Courtney H. Hodges. A few days later, the troops of the Second Byelorussian Front linked up with British army detachments along the Wismar-Schwerin-Wittenberg line. This was an extremely important event, particularly noted on April 27 in an order issued by Marshal Stalin, the Supreme Commander-in-Chief. On the occasion of the Soviet-American linkup, 324 artillery pieces fired a twenty-four-gun salute on Moscow's Red Square as a tribute to the gallant troops of the First Ukrainian Front and our Allies.

On April 25, U.S. President Harry Truman wrote to Joseph Stalin:

> The union of our arms in the heart of Germany has a meaning for the world which the world will not miss. . . . Nations which can plan and fight together shoulder to shoulder in the face of such obstacles of distance and of language and of communications as we have overcome

can live together and can work together in the common labor of the organization of the world for peace.

Hitler's hopes for discord between the Allies never came true. At the time, I unfortunately wasn't able to talk with our American allies, as I was busy dealing with Nazi counterattacks. Of our three corps that had reached the Elbe on April 23, two were being transferred to the army's left flank, where the German Görlitz Group had delivered a powerful blow. I learned of the linkup in the heat of battle, on April 25, in a telephone call to my observation post. It was only several days later—after the Görlitz Group had been stopped and defeated—that I was able to go to the Elbe.

I spent almost the entire day of April 30 with Gen. Hodges. More than thirty years have passed since then, but I still often think of Gen. Hodges. He was middle-aged—reserved, reticent, with an austere look about him. I found out later, however, that he was also kindhearted. Our conversations convinced me that he was a gifted military leader. His every gesture and word betrayed his joy over the victory.

Gen. Hodges paid us a visit, accompanied by his staff officers. After an official ceremony held in a large hall, we made introductory remarks, then talked at length about our mutual impressions of the war. Gen. Hodges and the other U.S. generals expressed admiration for the fortitude displayed by Soviet troops, the mass heroism they had demonstrated while on the defensive, and the enormous scale of the Soviet offensive. Our visitors were curious to learn how effective U.S. aid to the Soviet Union had been throughout the war. For instance, they wanted to know what U.S. weapons and equipment had been used by our Fifth Guards Army.

We thanked the Americans for their high opinion of our troops. As for the U.S. weapons, I described the situation exactly as it was. In 1942, we had received a few Valentine and Churchill tanks and some antiaircraft guns—not many. Our army had been supplied throughout the war primarily with Soviet weapons and machinery. We offered to take the Americans to any of our divisions so they could see for themselves what equipment we were using. We did, however, praise U.S. jeeps, pickups, and trucks, which had served us very well indeed, and we sincerely thanked the Americans for them.

During the dinner that followed, we toasted victory, friendship among nations, and a lasting peace. We also watched a performance given by our amateur army company. The Americans were especially delighted with Russian folk songs and dances. Gen. Hodges and I exchanged remarks. He said that this meeting between representatives of the Fifth Guards Army and the U.S. First Army was the happy day everyone had long awaited. He told us we had succeeded in defeating a more powerful enemy, that we had reached the heart of Germany and stepped across the Oder, which meant the defeat of Germany. He went on to say that the Americans would always remember the contribution which not only the Red Army itself, but also the Fifth Army, had made to the victory. Saying this, Gen. Hodges presented our Fifth Guards Army with an American flag which had been carried with U.S. troops all the way from America, across the Atlantic, to Britain, across the English Channel to Normandy, across France and Belgium to the very heart of Germany. He added that the flag was a token of his respect for me and for the officers of my army.

I thanked Gen. Hodges for his kind words for the Soviet armed forces, and said:

> On this long-awaited, happy day, when the armies of two great nations have met on the Elbe, we are proud of our alliance and our gallant fighting men. The glorious Red Army has fought long and hard. Together with its Allies, it has emerged victorious from this war, and is about to bring about the total defeat of Nazi Germany. May this meeting be a guarantee of a stable and lasting peace on our planet!

ALEXEI ZHADOV (1901E1977), was a prominent Soviet military leader who became a General of the Army in 1955. During the Great Patriotic War (World War II), he was an army commander, a post he held from 1942. After the war, Gen. Zhadov occupied various high-ranking positions in the Armed Forces of the USSR.

16. Grigori Goloborodko

"A group of soldiers wearing helmets and uniforms unlike those of the Germans appeared from behind buildings."

Lt. Grigori Goloborodko.

The road we took to the Elbe had been a long one. I served in the war from the very beginning up until its victorious end—1,418 days and nights. Behind us lay the bitter paths of retreat. Behind us lay Stalingrad and the Kursk Bulge . . . thousands of obstacles to cross—rivers and lakes, forests and swamps, mine fields and fortifications.

It wasn't an easy task commanding an infantry company, especially when you consider they were usually led by sergeants because there weren't enough officers. Company commanders inspired soldiers to action and often served as examples to the troops. Many of them fell on the battlefield. As a company commander myself, I had an acute sense of responsibility for my men and for their lives. A feeling I never lost.

Imagine how I felt when we were confronted by a barrier of water as large as the Elbe! At the time, I didn't have any idea that the river would become the meeting place for Soviet and American troops. We occupied the small town of Kreinitz on April 23, and continued fighting to break through to the river itself. The

Nazis met us with stiff resistance. Their order of battle was completely jumbled—the SS, *Gestapo*, *Volkssturm*, and troops of the *Hitlerjugend*. Rank-and-file soldiers were fighting alongside officers. Because we were on the offensive, we suffered heavy casualties. I had only a few of my men left, and reinforcements were hard to come by. Only on our own soil were we able to get new recruits from newly-liberated towns or villages.

It was only on April 24 that I learned there was the possibility of immediate contact with the Allies. Maj. Fyodor Glotov, commander of the Second Guards Infantry Battalion, ordered me to ready my company for a reconnaissance mission to the opposite bank of the Elbe. He added that we would receive further instructions from Lt. Col. Gordeyev, our regimental commander. I reminded him that the Company needed reinforcements to properly accomplish the mission . . .

On the morning of April 25, we crossed the Elbe under cover of fog. Because the enemy left us alone, we advanced unimpeded southwest toward the town of Strehla until we found a spot which was high and dry—a suitable observation post. We dug in and waited. The town looked dead, but we didn't dare enter it. After all, the Nazis were experienced combat soldiers, and we had learned not to take unnecessary risks. We sent out scouts to reconnoiter Strehla and its environs.

It was a sunny, warm day, the first day our men could walk around without crouching. The medals on their tunics glittered in the sunshine. We all felt that the war was over. They were moments of such happiness and hope—I'll remember them the rest of my life.

At about noon, we heard the rumble of engines. Because there was no sound of tracks, we assumed that the vehicles weren't tanks. We were right. We saw a group of soldiers driving into the town in jeeps, and figured they must be Americans when we saw their series of green flares.

Our regimental commander had alerted us that the Americans would use green flares for identification. And so we fired the prearranged series of red flares in response. A group of soldiers wearing helmets and uniforms unlike those of the Germans appeared from behind buildings. They were followed by cars driving out onto the highway which led to the Elbe. The cars were the final evidence we needed to confirm that the men were Americans—they were driving jeeps, like those in our division.

After a while, I tried to exchange information concerning our location with an American lieutenant. But we couldn't understand each other. Then I faced the lieutenant in the direction of the Elbe, pointed to Kreinitz, then showed where we were on my map. We understood each other and broke out laughing.

I learned the name of the American lieutenant some time later, when Lt. Col. Gordeyev invited him and his reconnaissance men to visit our regiment. He was Albert ("Buck") Kotzebue. I also met that day with Pfc. Joseph Polowsky, but we became friends only ten years later, in 1955, when he visited Moscow, and we swore once more to do our best to prevent another war.

GRIGORI GOLOBORODKO (1912-1958) was born in the Ukrainian village of Salovka in the Kremenchug District, Poltava Region. In 1935, he enlisted in the Red Army. He was transferred to the Front in 1941. After the war, Goloborodko returned to his native village, where he worked as a machine operator on a collective farm.

17. ALEXANDER GORDEYEV

"The refugees—especially the women, children, and old people—were a pitiful sight."

On April 18, 1945, the 175th Infantry Division, advancing in the vanguard of the Fifty-eighth Infantry Division, crossed the Spree west of Weisswasser. We were approaching Berlin when our division received orders to break through to the Elbe in the vicinity of Torgau-Riesa, seize the crossings there, and hold the east bank, thereby averting an enemy retreat. After briefly discussing the assignment with my battalion commanders and deputies, I decided to motorize my infantry—employing some of the vehicles captured from the Germans—and move rapidly toward the Elbe while avoiding protracted combat with the enemy. In so doing, I intended to use the division's second echelon to block enemy troops in urban areas.

Because the Germans were putting up no resistance in the west, our Allies were advancing virtually unhampered. In the meantime, we had to break fierce enemy opposition, particularly that of the SS *Leibstandarte Adolf Hitler Division*, which had been hastily transferred to our sector of the Front. Thus it turned out that on April 23, as it was repulsing SS counterattacks, the Second Infantry Battalion of the 175th Infantry Regiment under the command of Maj. Glotov penetrated to the right bank of the Elbe east of Strehla. Having beaten back an enemy now in retreat, Glotov's battalion seized a crossing of the Elbe. The battalion was soon joined by the rest of the regiment. The Command Post was established in the little town of Kreinitz, four kilometers northeast of Strehla. My own observation post was in the belfry of a church, where our communications men had installed a telephone line.

Late on the night of April 23, we exchanged fire with enemy troops across the Elbe. Fierce fighting raged near Riesa from April 24 until the next morning. The first thing our communications men did was exchange information with nearby military units. It was at this time that Maj. Gen. Rusakov, our division commander who was then at the 173rd Infantry Regiment's observation post, alerted me to possible contact with the Americans. He told me that green flares fired on the west bank of the river would mean "We are your Allies" and that we should fire red flares in response. Briefing me on a reconnaissance mission which was to be carried out on the left bank of the Elbe, Rusakov advised me to find an officer or soldier with a command of English, and to take him along. We were given the order not to open mortar or artillery fire on left-bank settlements until it was definitely established who was holding them. The crossing of the Elbe was noted in an Order of the Day issued by Col. Gen. Zhadov, commander of the Fifth Guards Army. It said, "In penetrating to the Elbe, in areas with no Allied troops on the west bank, seize the crossings and bridgeheads and hold them."

By noon of April 24, action had come to a standstill. Silence at the Front has a disquieting effect, and I told my division commander of my apprehensions. He told me to send out a reconnaissance party across the Elbe the next morning—April 25—and to instruct my men to hold their fire and go no farther than ten kilometers west of the river bank. I entrusted the mission to the Sixth Infantry Company under Senior Lt. Grigori Goloborodko.

They crossed the river early on the morning of April 25. Encountering no resistance, they proceeded to a location one kilometer north of Strehla. At 11:30 A.M., Goloborodko radioed that they had sighted a group of soldiers in unfamiliar uniforms. I ordered them to fire several red flares—the agreed-upon signal. They did so, and saw a series of green flares fired in reply. Shortly thereafter, Goloborodko reported having made contact with a group of U.S. soldiers. The Company had thus accomplished its mission, and I told them to bring the Americans over to the regiment's positions.

Sometime later, the Sixth Infantry Company and units attached to it returned to Kreinitz, bringing with them a few members of the U.S. patrol. They arrived at 1:30 P.M. I reported the contact to our division commander, and he instructed me to give the visitors a warm welcome. The division commander was represented by his Chief of Staff—Col. Rudnik, Maj. Anatoly Ivanov, and other officers. I went with my deputies—Yakov Kozlov, Tosoltan Bitarov, and Vladimir Lysov—to the ferry-crossing where we met the Americans. They were a patrol of the 273rd Infantry Regiment of the U.S. Sixty-ninth Infantry Division led by Lt. Kotzebue. Before long, we were joined by many of our men.

The meeting was really exciting. The U.S. soldiers looked respectfully at our Guards insignia and medals, asked us what they were and what the red and yellow stripes on our tunics meant. When we told them the stripes denoted wounds, they expressed their admiration for the heroism of Soviet soldiers. Soon bottles of Russian vodka and simple snacks appeared on the army capes that had been spread on the lawn. The Soviet and American soldiers drank to a world without war and to our friendship sealed by the blood which had been shed during our common struggle against the enemy. Pfc. Joseph Polowsky, a handsome and emotional man who turned out to be the deputy commander of the U.S. patrol, was the friendliest American in the party. He could speak German, so he talked to us through an interpreter. He warmly thanked the Soviet troops for their decisive contribution to the defeat of our common enemy. He also said he would like the Americans and Russians always to be friends.

Polowsky asked me for a photograph, but I didn't have one on me. Fortunately, Lt. Col. Yakov Kozlov had a group photo of the 175th Regiment's commanding officers, and I was only too glad to sign it and give it to Joseph Polowsky.

Our first meeting over, it was time to return to other matters. In particular, we had to take care of the German refugees. An enormous number of civilians who had been driven from the eastern part of Germany as a consequence of the Nazi Command's evacuation order, civilians who had been given no chance of crossing the river, had gathered on the east bank of the Elbe, especially at Kreinitz, but all that was left of the local ferry service was a cable strung across the river. Many German officers and soldiers wearing civilian clothes were in the crowd. The refugees—especially the women, children, and old people—were a pitiful sight. We had our field kitchens cook them a simple meal, after which we cared for the sick and wounded. It was clear to us that they should be returned to their homes as soon as possible.

We met the Americans again the following day—April 26. Members of Lt. Kotzebue's and Maj. Craig's patrols crossed the river and landed at Kreinitz. Among them were Albert Kotzebue himself, Pfc. Joseph Polowsky, and soldiers Carl Robinson, Elijah Sams, Byron Shiver, Charles Forrester, and Murry Schulman. Our men gave them a cordial reception.

ALEXANDER GORDEYEV was born in 1916 in the village of Drozhevo, Vladimir Region, in the Russian Soviet Federated Socialist Republic. He enlisted in the Army in 1937. Commissioned in 1939, he fought from the first to last day of the war, taking part in the Battles of Moscow and Stalingrad, the Battle of Berlin, combat at the Elbe and in Prague. As deputy chief of his regimental staff, he was in charge of reconnaissance. He later became a regimental commander. Col. Gordeyev was wounded five times and shell-shocked twice. In 1962, he retired from the Army as a partially-disabled veteran. He is married, and has both children and grandchildren.

(*Novosti Press*)

Sgt. Olshansky visits his village in the Ukraine.

18. ALEXANDER OLSHANSKY

*"We were covered from head to foot with
spring mud."*

The Red Army liberated my Ukrainian village of
Olshany from the Nazis in December 1942. During the occupation, the enemy had plundered and
burned thousands of Ukrainian towns and vil-
lages and taken many of their young people to Germany to work
in forced-labor camps. Among them was my sister, Nina, an
elementary school teacher. My father, elder sister Maria, and her
husband were serving at the Front.

I was only seventeen years old when I joined the Fifty-eighth
Infantry Division. At the time of the Elbe linkup, I held the rank of
sergeant. From the Don to the Elbe, I covered many thousands of
meters under enemy fire, often crawling or sprinting. I was

wounded three times and shell-shocked twice, but I knew that the way home lay through Berlin.

The Vistula-Oder Offensive paved our way to the Elbe and Berlin. At the request of President Roosevelt and Prime Minister Churchill—both of whom wanted us to help the Allies with their complicated situation on the Western Front—our division launched the Offensive against the Nazis on January 12, 1945— earlier than had been originally planned. From that date, our division fought with ferocity and traversed hundreds of kilometers, thereby making its unquestioned supremacy keenly felt.

As we were approaching the German border, we naturally longed for retribution. This instilled the Nazis with mortal terror— they knew only too well what crimes they had committed on Soviet soil. We did realize, however, that it was not the German people who were to be held responsible for the evil deeds of the Nazi leaders and of their tools—the SS, *Gestapo*, the punitive detachments, and other killers—for the people had been deceived by Nazi propaganda.

The Nazi generals had succeeded in maintaining the organized resistance of their troops in the East. They had declared that in all areas west of the Oder, every German had to defend his own home. It was then, for the first time during the war, that Nazi officers and enlisted men fought alongside the *Gestapo*, SS troops, the police, military cadets, old men, and even teenagers. They would retreat at night, moving from one town to the next. In the daytime, they would fortify a position in a stone house or cellar and continue fighting with the stubbornness of those condemned to death. Although we ourselves suffered significant casualties as we were advancing westward, we were still optimistic, for we felt the war was coming to an end.

The closer we got to the Elbe, the fiercer enemy resistance became. All roads leading to bridges and river crossings were crowded with retreating German troops and refugees. Goebbels's propaganda machine had so frightened the populace that many civilians were rushing westward across the Elbe.

On April 23, our regiment reached the town of Kreinitz, then proceeded to the river crossings. We posted sentries, dug in, and slept peacefully for the first time in many days, knowing that because the bridges and other crossings had already been blown by the Nazis, the enemy could not attack us from the front.

However, scattered groups of German troops to our rear would now and then open fire on us. They were armed SS men in civilian clothes who were doggedly forcing their way across the Elbe, sparing no one in their path.

The town of Kreinitz lies about five kilometers northeast of Strehla. On the morning of April 24, the area lay in a deep fog. By noon, it had cleared, and we were finally able to distinguish the shore of the left bank and the dams along the river. In the distance, beyond the marshes, was a highway on which a lone car would pass now and then. Realizing the necessity of reconnoitering the opposite river bank, our regimental commander ordered his infantry battalion commanders to conduct a reconnaissance mission there. To do so, they had to find locations for fords, and prepare crossing facilities. Senior Lt. Fyodor Verkhoturov and his platoon of combat engineers started looking for logs to make a raft. By that time, all the infantry battalion commanders had been alerted to the possibility that they might make contact with U.S. troops. They were informed of the agreed-upon identification signals.

On the morning of April 25, the Sixth Infantry Company of the 175th Infantry Regiment under the command of Grigori Goloborodko crossed the Elbe to determine the potential and composition of the enemy troops then holding the left bank of the river. I was then in charge of the company's communications. We advanced without encountering any resistance and dug in near Strehla. We soon heard the hum of engines, and saw a group of helmeted men—armed and dressed in strange uniforms. As we later learned, it was a patrol of the Fifth Army Corps of the First Army.

At first, we felt a little embarrassed, for we were covered from head to foot with spring mud—we'd been lying in trenches for quite some time. Our tunics and trousers were threadbare at the elbows and knees because we often had to crawl on our bellies. The Americans had come by jeep. Although their uniforms were somewhat cleaner, their faces were unshaven, just like ours.

The Americans were amazed that we wore no helmets. We explained that we had taken them off in the early days of the offensive for a simple reason. Although helmets provided good protection for troops on the defensive, they were of no use when you were in trenches, for they were vulnerable to both bullets and shrapnel. Helmets were also heavy, and tended to block your view.

Addressing Goloborodko, the American patrol commander said he was Albert Kotzebue. And then we—Soviet and American soldiers—met like friends, like comrades in arms, and warmly shook hands. This occurred at 11:30 A.M., Moscow time. Lt. Kotzebue sent ten of his men in two jeeps back to his HQ to report the contact. The rest of the patrol—eleven soldiers in three jeeps—stayed with him. Goloborodko also reported the meeting to the regimental commander, who invited the U.S. reconnaissance men to visit his Command Post in Kreinitz.

Kotzebue found a boat which was chained to the shore. He blew up the chain with a hand grenade and crossed the river in the boat with two of his men. Our combat engineers met the American lieutenant and his soldiers, and took them to regimental HQ. Pfc. Joseph Polowsky and his men made a raft from inflatable rubber boats, and also crossed the Elbe, moving along the steel cable, which was all that remained of a destroyed German ferry.

As they arrived at regimental HQ, the Americans were welcomed by its commander, Lt. Col. Alexander Gordeyev, by his deputies Lt. Cols. Yakov Kozlov and Tosoltan Bitarov, and by others. We invited the guests to dinner. In the afternoon, while the party was in full swing, another U.S. reconnaissance patrol led by Maj. Fred Craig arrived at HQ. In the evening, Lt. Kotzebue and three of his men drove back to their own positions. At his request, eight other Americans and their three jeeps remained with us overnight. They were given beds and food.

According to the Regiment's *War Diary*, the meeting passed "in a cordial atmosphere . . . The Americans thanked us for our friendly welcome and fraternal attitude. The day of our linkup with the Allies became a celebration of the triumph over Fascism . . ."

MAJ. GEN. ALEXANDER OLSHANSKY was born in 1925. During the Great Patriotic War, he served as a rank-and-file soldier with the same regiment as it advanced from the Don to the Elbe. After the war, he pursued a military career, and eventually attained the rank of general. Now retired from the Army, he is a department head at Moscow's Institute of Railway Transport. Maj. Gen. Olshansky is an Honorary Citizen of Dallas, Texas, and the state of Kansas.

19. LYUBOV KOZINCHENKO (ANDRYUSHCHENKO)

*"The two of us—
members of the most
humane profession—
were the first to greet
each other on that
historic day."*

(Novosti Press)

My generation was a war generation, although we didn't want that war and still curse it. I enlisted for front-line duty in 1942 along with nine of my girlfriends. We served as field nurses and medical assistants with the 175th Infantry Regiment. Our journey on the long roads of war was a difficult one. As dangerous as they were for the men, they were even more dangerous for us women. Indeed, carrying the wounded at the Front while under shellfire was much more hazardous than serving in HQs or field hospitals. We girls had to do this right under the enemy's nose while being shot at by Nazi infantry, machine gunners, and particularly the snipers, who totally ignored the red crosses on our white armbands. Many, far too many nurses were killed in action during the war.

Sometimes, we had to give first aid to enemy soldiers as well. During the 1942-1943 offensive, for example, many Italian and German soldiers fighting at Stalingrad would have frozen to death in the snow had it not been for Soviet nurses. I still remember the hard time we had in February of 1942 near the Lozovaya railway station in the Ukraine. Our battalion's first-aid posts and the regiment's medical company station were overflowing with wounded we couldn't evacuate because the Nazis had surrounded us. Fortunately, a platoon of submachine gunners was with us guarding the regimental banner. Also present was Maj. Alexei Shapovalov, the regiment's Chief of Staff, as well as his officers. They had some carts at their disposal. We destroyed everything we didn't need and loaded our wounded into the empty carts. Late that night, our soldiers launched a surprise attack against the enemy, and broke out of the trap.

At the time, none of us dreamed we would one day contact our Allies in the very heart of Nazi Germany, near the Elbe. Of course, it's not just those who participated in the linkup of April 25, 1945, who deserve the credit. That meeting was made possible by all those who had fought in defense of the Brest Fortress, of Moscow and Stalingrad, by those who reached—and didn't reach—Berlin.

I myself shall never forget the day of the linkup. It was the first real day of spring, full of sunlight and happiness, with no wounded to care for, no shooting, no deaths. From the very first day of the offensive which had brought us to the Elbe, which had begun on January 12, 1945, we'd forced our way through the fierce resistance of the enemy army, *Volkssturm*, and the kids of the *Hitler jugend* . . .

We learned of our possible contact with the Allies on the morning of April 25 when Senior Lt. Goloborodko reported contact from the west bank of the Elbe. We got busy, seeing to the preparation of dinner and gathering flowers for the Allies. Goloborodko himself soon arrived, and we congratulated him on his contact with a U.S. reconnaissance group. We decided the war was at last over, and began congratulating each other on the victory.

At about noon, we descended the steep embankment of the Elbe until we reached the crossing at the southern outskirts of Kreinitz. The young Americans had made a raft of inflated rubber boats which traveled quickly along a steel cable strung across the river. Not far from the landing, combat engineers under the command of Senior Lt. Fyodor Verkhoturov were waiting to meet the Americans. The first American to step onto the river bank was Carl L. Robinson, a field medical assistant. A big red cross was painted on his helmet. It so happened that I, a Soviet field nurse, had the honor of presenting my U.S. medical colleague with a bouquet of flowers. Thus, the two of us—members of the most humane profession—were the first to greet each other on that historic day.

The American soldiers were dressed in combat uniforms—well-worn cotton khaki coats and matching pants worn over high boots. Lt. Kotzebue's coat was burnt in one spot, his collar unbuttoned. He smoked his pipe, from which he never parted.

The following day, April 26, the American soldiers who came to meet us were wearing full dress uniform made of a woolen material. Only the members of the reconnaissance patrol led by Maj. Craig were still wearing their field tunics. Those U.S. soldiers had spent the night at our position.

Our meeting with the Americans were friendly, cheerful, and imbued with a feeling of trust. All of us were anticipating the end of the war. Every U.S. soldier wanted to have some memento of our meeting, so we parted not only with the stars from our caps and epaulets, but also with our buttons. The language barrier which had been a problem the first day vanished on the second. Some of the Americans, as well as prisoners of war who had been liberated from the Nazi camps, could speak Russian. By then, many interpreters and reporters had also arrived.

That's what I remember about the linkup of Soviet and American soldiers on the Elbe, the soldiers who had fought courageously—side by side—against a common enemy.

LYUBOV KOZINCHENKO (ANDRYUSHCHENKO) was born in 1922 in the city of Boguchar, Voronezh Region. She went to the Front as a field nurse in 1942. After the war, she worked for the BogucharBoard of Public Health. She is married, and has children and grandchildren.

(Novosti Press)

Comedians Timoshenko and Berezin in action for American troops. (see p. 171)

20. ALEXANDER GRIGORASHCHENKO

"We rushed to see them."

The Nazis occupied Bolshaya Viska, the Ukrainian village where I was born and grew up, in the very first months of the war. Until March 1944, I lived in occupied territory. The whole world knows what atrocities the Nazis committed in our land. After our liberation by the Red Army, I went to the Front as a communications man for a mortar battery.

In April 1945, I along with the other men of my regiment took part in a meeting with Americans from the 273rd Infantry Regiment of the U.S. Sixty-ninth Division. I wasn't one of those who actually crossed the Elbe, but I'd heard that the infantry company under Grigori Goloborodko—whom I knew well—had met the Americans in the morning. When the Americans came to visit us, we rushed to see them. I was told that one of them was an American general—a division commander—but I couldn't identify him. There was no mistaking division commanders in the Red Army. Soviet generals usually wore trousers with red stripes, shoulder straps with big, shiny stars, and a general's cap.

I walked up to an American who was with an interpreter, thinking that maybe he could point out the General to me. At that very moment, our division commander, Vladimir Rusakov, walked past us with a tall, sturdy, middle-aged American at his side. On his helmet were to big stars beneath a large number—"69." I was told that was Gen. Emil Reinhardt of the U.S..

As I was talking to the American, someone photographed me. Only recently did I learn that the man I was talking to was Lt. Kotzebue.

ALEXANDER GRIGORASHCHENKO was born in the Kirovograd Region of the Ukraine in 1922. Grigorashchenko served in a mortar company from April 1944 until Victory Day. After the war, he returned home and worked on a collective farm.

21. PAVEL RUDENKO

"They'd used them only as can openers."

My heart aches whenever I think of my comrades in arms who fell on the long road from the Volga to the Elbe and Berlin, who perished in Nazi slavery or were burned in the furnaces of Majdanek or Auschwitz.

I was an infantry captain, commander of a battalion. On April 23, 1945, we broke through to the Elbe along a wide sector of the Front extending from Riesa in the south to Torgau in the northwest. My battalion was fighting at the division's left flank. My assignment was to secure the limiting point with the Fiftieth Infantry Regiment of the Fifteenth Infantry Division. Our regiment's Second Infantry Battalion, commanded by my friend Maj. Fyodor Glotov, was fighting to our right.

On the morning of April 25, the Sixth Infantry Company of his battalion met a reconnaissance patrol of the U.S. Sixty-ninth Infantry Division while reconnoitering the opposite bank of the Elbe. That same day, at a dinner party hosted by the regiment, I met Lt. Albert Kotzebue and his men. It was truly a great occasion. In no time flat, we found a common language. The young and sociable Americans had arrived in their jeeps. They were carrying their rifles tipped with bayonets. We asked them if they'd ever used their bayonets in combat. They laughingly told us, no, they'd used them only as can openers.

Yes, the blood shed by Soviet and American soldiers in their common struggle against Nazi Germany and militarist Japan sealed their friendship. It was a friendship born and strengthened on the battlefields of World War II. It's still alive. The postwar reunions of the veterans of both countries are the best proof of that!

PAVEL RUDENKO was born in 1910. He graduated from an infantry school in 1942, and was sent to the Front. After the war, he became a schoolteacher. He and his family live in Kurgan, in the Urals.

(*Novosti Press*)

22. TOSOLTAN BITAROV

"I still remember our men joking about the Americans being 'taken prisoner' by the Russians."

The day Nazi Germany treacherously invaded the Soviet Union was my twenty-first birthday. At the time, I was a cadet at the Podolsk Machine Gunners' Training School near Moscow. My birthday party was canceled because of the war. That same day, I received the last birthday telegram from my family, which lived far away—in Northern Ossetia.

In August 1941, all of us cadets graduated as lieutenants and were sent to the Front. I was appointed commander of a machine gun company at the Kalinin Front. Our retreat was a very bitter experience. During the fighting near Moscow, I was severely wounded for the first time and had to spend more than two months in a hospital. After my recovery, I was assigned to the Fifty-eighth Guards Infantry Division. In March 1943, I became deputy commander of the 175th Infantry Regiment. This was the rank I held when we reached the Elbe.

At nine o'clock on the morning of April 24, 1945, the Fifteenth Division's Fiftieth Infantry Regiment, under the command of Maj. Medvedev, crossed the Elbe near a railway bridge not far from Riesa. Its assignment was to seize a bridgehead, enter the city, and smash the enemy artillery. The fighting was long and fierce. By the end of the day, the regiment had driven the enemy from the outskirts of the city and captured the bridgehead on the west bank of the river. But the regiment had failed to take the city itself. Throughout the day, the counterattacks of the Görlitz Group had increased with greater frequency.

On the morning of April 25, the Nazis brought up reinforcements—as many as two infantry battalions, three artillery, and

Soviets greet Kotzebue patrol at Kreinitz.

(*Novosti Press*)

three mortar batteries—from Strehla to the northern edges of Riesa. The enemy launched two counterattacks, each involving two hundred men and three self-propelled guns. We repulsed both attacks. Although we had to fight for every house in the city in order to break the Nazis' stiff resistance, Riesa was ours by the end of the day. However, the Germans made several futile attempts to recapture the bridgehead held by the Fiftieth Regiment.

At noon on the 25th, the reconnaissance patrol led by Lt. Kotzebue arrived at our regimental HQ. We met the Americans on the pier of the ferry-crossing near Kreinitz. At four o'clock—as the meeting between the U.S. patrol and our regimental commanders, representatives of division HQ, and our reporters was in full swing—a second group of Americans arrived at the Kreinitz ferry. They were commanded by Maj. Fred Craig. The major told us that neither the U.S. division stationed at the Mulde nor the regiment that had sent the Kotzebue patrol on its reconnaissance mission to Strehla had as yet heard from it, and had become worried. The Lieutenant's radio hadn't been answering their calls. Aircraft had been sent out to find the patrol but had failed. It had then been decided to send out a search party led by Craig to the outskirts of Strehla to find Kotzebue and his men. This second patrol had left its regiment's positions at 3:00 P.M. on April 25. On their way to Strehla, Craig and his men had met the two jeeps which Kotzebue had sent back to his HQ to report the linkup.

After exchanging information with Kotzebue's men, Craig's group traveled in their seven jeeps to the Elbe. As they approached Strehla, they encountered a Soviet calvary detachment consisting of twenty mounted men and one motorcyclist. This was the vanguard detachment of the First Cavalry Corps commanded by Lt. Gen. Viktor Baranov. Because the cavalrymen knew nothing about the identification signals, they didn't give any information concerning their units to Craig's group. They shook hands and were photographed together. Some ten minutes later, the Americans arrived at Strehla's main square. They asked the locals for directions to the Soviet commandant's headquarters, and found out there wasn't one in town.

After a brief stop, the jeeps drove along the main street of Strehla, then on to the Elbe river bank, where they met troops and combat engineers of our 175th Regiment. Our men told the Americans that Lt. Kotzebue's reconnaissance patrol had crossed the Elbe at noon, and was in Kreinitz at that very moment. Craig's patrol also crossed the river to Kreinitz and participated in the meeting.

Several men of Kotzebue's reconnaissance patrol and Craig's search party spent the night at our regiment's position. Many enemy groups, both large and small, were still to our rear. They had refused to surrender. We subsequently posted a guard outside the house where the Americans were staying. When Maj. Craig and his men woke up early the next morning, they discovered one of our submachine gunners standing outside. They concluded we were holding them in custody. The U.S. soldiers distracted the sentries with conversation and insignificant requests while their officer sneaked out a window into the backyard. He left the area unnoticed, and reached an Anglo-American POW camp recently liberated by Soviet troops.

Sometime later, a U.S. regimental HQ got in touch with Lt. Col. Gordeyev and asked for Maj. Craig. We couldn't find him anywhere. The Americans phoned again half an hour later, then called a few more times. Before long, the U.S. HQ became suspicious, and told us they were sending a representative to meet with us.

Gordeyev sent his men out to look for the American officer and bring him back. He himself drove to the POW camp. But it was in

the commandant's office that he finally found the missing major—
fast asleep after the banquet. By that time, the American
representative had arrived on the scene. Gordeyev took him to the
camp and thus resolved the misunderstanding. I still remember our
men joking about the Americans being "taken prisoner" by the
Russians . . .

TOSOLTAN BITAROV was born in 1920 in Sadon, Northern Ossetia. He
is Ossetian. Bitarov fought at the Front from August 1941 until the end of
the war. He was seriously wounded three times. In 1946, he returned
home, where he became a school principal, then a mine foreman, and
eventually a section head. Bitarov is a fourth-generation miner; his family
has worked in the mines of Ossetia for more than three centuries. He is
married, and has children and grandchildren.

23. Alexei Baranov

"We communicated mostly through gestures and mime."

When I look at photos of the war, I'm reminded of the days of the linkup between our Fifty-eighth Infantry Division and the U.S. Sixty-ninth Division on the banks of the Elbe River. It was a meeting we had long looked forward to. For the nearly four years we'd been fighting from the Don and Volga to the Elbe, there had been one constant hope—that we would link up with the Allies to achieve final victory.

The snapshots show both the living and dead—those who fell in action or who died after the war. They're pictures of the men with whom I shared the hardships of war, its joys and triumphs, whom I ate with out of the same mess kit and shared a pup tent. Our division's infantry covered about five thousand kilometers, most of them in short spurts or by crawling on our bellies, seldom walking just normally. Many of my friends didn't live to see the linkup on the Elbe in 1945.

Some photos get me particularly excited, for they're of unforgettable events. One of them is of our first meeting with the Americans at the Elbe. I remember it so well, because those of us in communications learned all the news before anyone else did. At the time, I was a Top Sergeant in charge of a communications platoon, and could always tell by the tone of the commanders' voices if something important was in the air. Front-line soldiers used to say that the predictions of a communications man always come true.

Our division was fighting its way to Berlin when the order came through to penetrate to the Elbe right away. That meant we had to get our communications facilities ready and lay a telephone cable across the bottom of the river. It was a good thing we had solid experience laying communication lines across water. The most memorable had been the crossing of the Dnieper, which we had to do under heavy enemy fire. So as you can see, the platoon was quite capable of laying a cable across the bottom of the Elbe. In the meantime, the Germans' organized resistance hadn't let up. Besides that, groups of retreating Nazis fighting to our rear were doing everything they could to break through to the Elbe and cross it. We were often engaged in fire fights with them.

Late on the night of April 23, we realized that the last of the German troops were fleeing across the Elbe—their resistance had weakened and their gunfire letting up. By noon of the next day, the front lines were quiet. We had almost finished laying the cables. The HQ of the 175th Regiment occupied the little town of Kreinitz, and our vanguard detachments penetrated to the Elbe and seized what remained of the ferries.

The observation post of our regimental commander, Alexander Gordeyev, was located on the outskirts of Kreinitz. Our cable worked well, connecting the regimental commander with the division commander and other regimental HQs. On April 25, Alexander Gordeyev sent a reconnaissance patrol under Senior Lt. Grigori Goloborodko across the Elbe. Some of the men of my squad went along.

A short time later, we learned that Goloborodko's patrol had met with the vanguard of the U.S. Army, and that they were on their way to us. When the U.S. soldiers led by Albert Kotzebue stepped on the east bank of the Elbe, our men gave them a warm welcome. Everyone who happened to be nearby was impatient to greet the Allies. The meeting was very friendly, although we communicated mostly through gestures and mime. A few of the Americans, though, spoke a little Russian. We communications men went off duty one by one to shake hands with the Americans, pat them on the back, and exchange souvenirs.

Our division continued to advance toward Dresden, but was soon ordered to redirect its route to Prague and give urgent support there. We were in Prague when Nazi Germany surrendered. I had the honor of being sent by the division command to take part in the Victory Parade held in Moscow on June 24, 1945.

ALEXEI BARANOV was born in 1913 in Medyn District, Smolensk Region, in the Russian Soviet Federated Socialist Republic. He went to the Front on the first day of the Great Patriotic War—June 22, 1941. After the war, Baranov was discharged from the Army and worked as the head of the Scientific and Technical Information Department at Moscow's Krasny Proletarii Machine-Tool Plant. He is married, and has children and grandchildren.

(Novosti Press)

U.S. and Soviet soldiers study map at Kreinitz.

24. Polina Nekrasova (Dushchenko)

"We realized for the first time in our combat experience there would be no blood bath on the Elbe."

B y the summer of 1942, Nazi troops had advanced as far as the Don and Volga. My girlfriends and I joined our combat soldiers as field nurses. We were just seventeen years old. We realized the life we'd chosen would be a difficult one. I'd already lost my mother, the person dearest to me. She'd died in the siege of Leningrad. My father was fighting at the Leningrad Front, my brother near Moscow.

My first combat experience took place on the Don. That memorable battle began with the frosty sunrise of December 16, 1942. Our company commander was Captain of the Medical Service Antonina Busenina. We administered first aid to the wounded right there on the battlefield amid intensive enemy bombing and artillery, mortar, and machine gun fire. Those who fought at the Front know how strong and courageous a person had to be to carry the wounded while under enemy fire.

We learned during our training course that the sooner the wounded were cared for the less blood they were likely to lose, the better their chances of survival would be. But how difficult it was to reach them quickly! Nazi snipers spared no one, not even nurses wearing a red cross.

Because the wounded were usually concentrated at bridge-heads, we could transport them to the medical unit's first-aid station only at night. The moment the Nazis saw boats and rafts carrying the wounded, they would sink them. The enemy did this on the Dnieper, Yuzhny Bug, Dniester, Vistula, Oder, Neisse, and Spree. We didn't know then that it would be different at the Elbe. To our great surprise, the Soviet troops which had penetrated to the Elbe didn't proceed across the river. It was only on the morning of April 25 when our soldiers met the Americans that we realized that for the first time in our combat experience there would be no blood bath on the Elbe.

We didn't know at the time that a friend of ours, nurse Lyuba Kozinchenko (now Andryushchenko) would be one of the participants of the Soviet-American linkup. She pinned a sprig of lilacs on the tunic of a U.S. soldier, Carl Robinson.

We nurses actually saw the Americans on April 26. They were young, handsome fellows, outgoing, but at the same time a little shy—perhaps because we'd just met. My girlfriends and I also felt very shy each time one of them asked us to dance.

But the celebrations didn't last long. We were given new orders, resumed fighting, and continued taking care of the wounded all the way to Prague. We were there when Germany surrendered. For us, the war ended in Czechoslovakia on May 12.

I'm glad I survived and became a mother and grandmother.

POLINA NEKRASOVA (DUSHCHENKO) was born in 1925 in the village of Glubokoye, Voronezh Region, in the Russian Soviet Federated Socialist Republic. She completed nine years of secondary education before the outbreak of the war. In December 1942, Nekrasova served as a medic in the Battle of Stalingrad. She was shell-shocked at the town of Boguchar. For her wartime heroism, she received numerous military decorations. At the end of the war, Nekrasova was employed as a telephone operator. Today she lives in the city of Kaliningrad.

25. ALEXANDER SILVASHKO

*"Tears streamed down the face of this
hardened soldier."*

When the war came to the Ukraine in 1941, I was
working in a Komsomol regional committee. Like
so many others, I experienced the horrors of the
Nazi occupation. Because I wasn't old enough to
enlist—only seventeen—I was evacuated with the others to the
rear. But although I couldn't yet join the Red Army, I fought the
enemy all the same as a partisan. On December 12, 1942, I took my
official oath as a soldier. The first place I saw combat duty was on
the Don. The last was in Prague.

Soon after enlisting, I was assigned to the Eighth Rifle Company
of the 173rd Rifle Regiment. My machine gun platoon advanced
with the regiment's forward units. When the war ended, I was still
with the same platoon as its senior lieutenant. I was wounded
twice, shell-shocked once. But after I'd recovered from my

(*Novosti Press*)

143

144 ★★ YANKS MEET REDS

injuries, I returned from the hospital straight to my platoon. Combat on the Don, combat beyond the Dnieper, the siege of the Bug—those were particularly hard times, bloody days. And when we reached Germany itself? What a fight the enemy put up there! The fascists held out in every way possible—dead or alive. But we were victorious!

What can I say about our meeting with the Americans in April 1945? To break through to the Elbe River, our troops had to cover a great distance, had to cross rivers and pass through vast woods and across marshes, mine fields, and various fortifications. My own platoon met with desperate and often fierce resistance on the part of scattered German troops. We had to smash the enemy's defenses—giving it no chance of regrouping—and crush any reinforcements. In so doing, our troops showed amazing heroism and courage. And as we defeated the Nazis, we liberated many thousands of people from various European countries imprisoned in death camps.

We were approaching the city of Torgau late on April 24, fighting to knock out the enemy bridgeheads there. My platoon was in the lead. The regiment's special detachments and horse-drawn logistical support units were following the main force. Having detected our battalion on the outskirts of the city, the Nazis bombarded us with artillery and mortar fire. We had to dig in and send out a reconnaissance patrol to survey the Nazi defenses. Having accomplished our mission, we forced the enemy out of its bridgeheads on April 25.

Fate would have it that Soviet and American troops would meet at the Elbe that day. It was a really special day, and I've never forgotten. It was springtime, warm and sunny. The lilacs were already in bloom. The early-morning fog on the Elbe cleared, and firing from the opposite bank ceased. All of us felt that the war was coming to an end. Walking along the girders of the blown-up bridge, my platoon crossed the Elbe to its western bank. Shortly thereafter, we returned to the east bank. In the meantime, Lt. Mikhail Chizhikov's scouts had gone on a reconnaissance mission to Torgau.

April 25 didn't begin with any meetings, but with savage fighting between the fascists and us. After we'd returned to the east bank, they tried to ambush us in the worst possible way. Fascist officers there in Torgau—women were even among them—walked out onto the bridge from the opposite bank of the river. All of them were wearing white armbands. We knew that white armbands meant that they wanted to surrender. For that reason, we waved them in our direction, as if saying, "Come on over. No one's going to shoot." They even called to us. The bridge had been broken. For this reason, we crawled across the girders toward them. A machine gunner went along with us. The Hitlerites soon opened fire, furious gunfire. It turned out that each of them was armed. We returned the fire. It was a terrible battle. I consider it a miracle I'm still alive . . .

Sometime later, a group of soldiers wearing unfamiliar uniforms appeared on the outskirts of Torgau. I thought this was going to be another ambush attempt. In the meantime, they'd started fastening some kind of flag to a church tower. Four soldiers soon appeared. It became apparent that they were Americans. We began talking back and forth, although we didn't know each other's language. But the resourcefulness we had as soldiers helped us figure out what was going on. The Americans yelled "Moscow," "America," and "Don't shoot!" We finally realized these men were our allies. To make a long story short, we began crawling across the bridge toward each other. We met in the middle. We shook hands. I saw that one of them was an officer. He said, "I'm William Robertson." I likewise introduced myself, saying I was "Guards Lt. Silvashko." I didn't know English, he didn't know Russian, so we spoke with gestures. But we both knew we had to report the situation to our superiors. Robertson asked us to take him to our regimental commander, then invited us to his division so he could prove he had really met the Russians.

We all gave a special sigh of relief. Our soldiers rushed to the river. We began washing ourselves and shaving. Someone tried to dunk himself in the cold water. It was a time of immense pleasure, joy. I remember how a machine gunner came up to me. He was the oldest soldier among us—almost fifty. He reminisced about his family. He talked about Kharkhov, about his village. The night before, he'd received a letter—his daughter was getting married. Tears streamed down the face of this hardened soldier. He'd been waiting for the victory, getting as close to it as he could.

As soon as I said I'd met the Americans, Maj. Larionov—the deputy regimental commander—came rushing to my trench along with combat Capt. Nyeda and party organizer Andreyev. In reply to Robertson's invitation, the four of us left in his jeep for a meeting at the American division headquarters. It was far away—about forty-five kilometers—and took us about an hour to get there.

Along the way, we saw German units that had been defeated by our troops choking the roads on their way to surrender to the Americans. Some German officers and men stopped our car and asked the way to the POW assembly points. They were amazed to see us sitting in the car right next to the Americans. Wearing medals and carrying arms, the Germans were surprisingly cheerful. They were moving in a column directly toward the division headquarters. There they neatly laid down their rifles, automatic rifles, and machine guns. The "prisoners" themselves walked around freely, making themselves at home.

The four of us, armed only with our side arms, were afraid of being ambushed, especially by SS men. We arrived at the American regimental HQ in Wurzen late at night. Obviously, we hadn't been expected—we could tell this by the fuss and turmoil created by our arrival. After a brief period of confusion, we continued on our way to the American divisional HQ at Trebsen. They had previously been told of our coming by telephone. Even though it was very late at night, we received a cordial welcome. Our hosts were hospitable, and the general atmosphere happy and festive. Numerous reporters immediately set upon us. It took us quite a while to get rid of them and finally have supper. Lasting well into the morning, that supper turned out to be an early breakfast . . .

Maj. Gen. Emil F. Reinhardt, Commander of the Sixty-ninth Division, received us. We drank to the Soviet and American armies and to our two nations. After having a group photograph taken, we drove to the Elbe in thirteen jeeps, accompanied by the American division commanders who were expected to meet with their Soviet counterparts on the Soviet bank of the Elbe that very day—April 26.

ALEXANDER SILVASHKO was born in 1922 in the Cherkassy Region of the Ukraine. After the war, he became a schoolteacher. He is today the principal of a school in the Byelorussian village of Kolki.

(*Novosti Press*)

Gen. Rusakov and Gen. Reinhardt leading troops to celebrate in Torgau.

Gen. Reinhardt on his way across the
Elbe to meet the Russians. (*AP Photo*)

Gen. Rusakov leading his staff to meet Gen. Reinhardt.

(*Novosti Press*)

Soviet correspondent interviewing GIs at Kreinitz.   (*Novosti Press*

26. Mikhail Chizhikov

"Automobiles appeared on the horizon and moved in our direction."

Engaged in combat with the Nazis, our 173rd Regiment of the Fifty-eighth Guards Rifle Division crossed the Neisse River on April 16, 1945. I was commander of an infantry reconnaissance platoon. A radio operator and artillery-fire adjuster had been assigned to me at the time we were heading for the Elbe. The focus of our reconnaissance mission was Torgau. Lt. Col. Spiridon Rudnik, our division's Chief of Staff, told me that we were likely to meet U.S. troops.

In eight days and nights, we covered 140-160 kilometers. By late afternoon of April 24, we had reached the Elbe near the town of Torgau. We first reconnoitered the east bank of the river. We discovered a private estate, where we captured eleven Nazis in hiding. We interrogated them right there, and sent them to Regimental HQ.

Just before dawn on April 25, we heard a powerful explosion in the vicinity of the town as we were continuing to reconnoiter the area. Only after we'd reached the east bank of the river and looked through the fog could we see the blurred outline of a blown-up bridge. We determined that even though a section of the bridge between the girders had plunged into the water, we could still get across it to the other side of the river. As soon as the fog had lifted, we decided to cross to the west bank along the sections of the bridge still intact. Our radio operator and other members of the patrol remained behind on the east bank. The four of us who went were Pvt. Ivan Shisharin and Nikolai Babich, Sergeant Viktor Gavronsky and I.

We could still hear shooting in Torgau. As we were crossing the damaged girders of the bridge, Nazi machine guns opened fire. Enemy machine gun nests were positioned right at water's edge to the left and right of the bridge. Ducking enemy bullets, we continued moving forward, firing along the way. After a brief exchange of gunfire, we drove the enemy from their positions, and "caught hold of" the west bank of the river.

Taking our positions near the bridge, we discovered several boats. We sent two of them to the opposite shore, where they picked up the remaining members of the patrol, including the radio operator, and returned to the west bank.

The enemy didn't launch a counterattack. We entered the town, proceeding with caution, carefully studying every building. At one place, a group of about ten to fifteen Nazis attacked us. But the platoon members kept their heads, and instantly opened fire. The Nazis immediately retreated.

Finally, we reached the western edge of the town and cut off the road leading in from the west. We had accomplished our mission.

Just as dawn was breaking, we spotted some kind of fortress right in front of us. It turned out to be a POW camp. The guards, having heard the exchange of gunfire, had already fled. Soon a group of people came out of the fortress and approached us. Among them were Russians, Ukrainians, Belgians, Englishmen, and those of other nationalities. Without concealing their joy, they invited us to come into the fortress to join with them in marking their day of liberation. We couldn't do that right then, because the situation in the town itself was still unclear. Sometime later, prisoners returned—this time with food and alcohol they had found in town. Right there by the road, all of us joined in celebrating their liberation and the joyous meeting.

Our farewell was a warm one indeed. Bright-colored strips of cloth were already flying over the camp. I don't exactly remember what was on them, but apparently they were the flags of various countries.

It was bright daylight—about eight or nine o'clock in the morning—when automobiles appeared on the horizon and moved in our direction. I gave the order, "Don't fire until I say so!" That way I'd be able to know if this possibly was the meeting with the Allies. The vehicles got closer. We saw they didn't resemble German automobiles. They were jeeps. Soldiers wearing unfamiliar uniforms were riding in them. I stood straight up. The first car came to a halt. It was followed by three others. That's how we met

"The horse I gave Bradley was a handsome and well-trained Don stallion."
—Ivan Konyev (see p. 165)

27. GRIGORY PROKOPYEV

"Men on both sides of the river tossed their caps and helmets into the air."

(Novosti Press)

Torgau was deserted because its populace, frightened by Nazi propaganda, had fled to the west. Baby buggies and carts filled with personal belongings were standing on the bridge that had been blown up by the retreating Nazi troops.

I was a company commander of the combat engineers battalion of the Fifty-eighth Infantry Division. Serving with the engineer troops was both extremely difficult and most dangerous. A combat engineer was the first to advance and the last to retreat. They used to say that he could make only one mistake in his life. Indeed, laying and clearing mines, as well as handling explosives, could be fatal. Besides that, a combat engineer—while under enemy fire— invariably had to handle mines of unknown design. The slightest mistake or an undetected booby trap meant almost certain death.

Combat engineers assigned to cross a water barrier such as the Elbe had to have a great deal of nerve and tremendous stamina. The enemy would usually concentrate its gunfire at the crossing and the ferrying facilities. Consequently, every crossing was a virtual hell, with a sea of fire, ear-splitting explosions, and a wall of smoke. Pillars of water would rise ten meters and more. Bombs and shells would smash boats and pontoons into splinters. The noted Soviet poet Alexander Tvardovsky wrote about it:

Crossing over, crossing over! . . .
Some found memories, some found glory,
Some, the water's dark embrace,
not a vestige, not a trace."

On April 26—the day after our linkup with the Allies—the engineers of the Fifty-eighth Infantry Division were assigned to construct a boat crossing for the American soldiers. The Elbe was a wide, deep river with a rather fast current. Its waters were cold and murky.

Army jeeps carrying U.S. infantrymen appeared on the horizon and soon reached the steep west bank near the crossing site. Soviet soldiers were waiting for the guests on the east bank. Men on both sides of the river tossed their caps and helmets into the air and cheered loudly. Our combat engineers quickly took the Americans—numbering 150 to 200—across the river. We smiled happily, eyes shining. We hugged our allies and shook their hands. We actually understood each other quite well even though none of us could speak the others' language.

Far away from our own homelands, on the bank of a German river, we sang songs, cracked jokes, laughed, and reminisced together. All of us realized that in a few days the war would be over, and we would at last be able to celebrate our victory. It really didn't occur to us then that the Elbe linkup would be such a significant moment in the history of World War II. We didn't know then that it would become a symbol of peace and friendship among nations.

We thought we would be able to celebrate the end of the war at the Elbe, but that's not how it turned out. After the linkup, the Fifty-eighth Infantry Division had to turn southward to liberate Dresden and Prague. It was when we were in Prague that Europe's bloodiest war, which had lasted for more than five and a half years, at last came to an end! The loss of life had been appalling. In the three years leading up to Victory Day, the personnel of my own company had changed three times.

Half the men who left my village to go to war never returned.

PROFESSOR GRIGORY PROKOPYEV was born in Arkhangelsk in 1923. He was drafted into the Army in July 1941, enrolled in a military engineering school, and left for the Front after graduation. He fought in the Ukraine and in the Battle of Stalingrad. After the war, he graduated from an agricultural academy and then received a Ph.D. degree in Economics. Professor Prokopyev has been teaching in Moscow colleges for more than thirty years. He is an Honorary Citizen of Dallas, Texas, and the state of Kansas.

Soviet with British sentry at the Elbe.   (*Novosti Press*)

28. Gleb Baklanov

"The delicious aroma of food expertly prepared mingled with the scent of apple blossoms."

At the appointed hour on April 27, my automobile sped up to the east bank of the Elbe across from Torgau. The ferry with the American General's jeep on it was already in the middle of the river. A crowd was waiting for him on the sandbar below. I saw about two dozen cars and some forty military men on the opposite shore.

The ferry landed on the east bank with a soft thud. A few seconds later, Maj. Gen. Clarence R. Huebner—the tall, lean commander of the U.S. Fifth Army Corps—was giving me a firm handshake as he bared his large yellowish teeth in a beaming smile. We began walking up a sandy path. The staff officers who had come out to meet us stood at attention facing the river. Two men held a banner bearing a replica of the medal "For the Defense of Stalingrad." As previously arranged, the soldiers unfurled the banner at my command, and it fluttered in the spring breeze.

Although Gen. Huebner was by no means a young man—I think he was about sixty at the time—he easily climbed the slope, his weather-beaten face becoming slightly flushed and his breathing a little deeper. We stopped and faced the officers standing at attention. Addressing Gen. Huebner, I said, "General, please accept this modest memento of our historic linkup on the banks of the Elbe, a symbol of the friendship between the Allies fighting against Nazism." Pointing to the banner, I continued, "This is not a standard, but a flag depicting the medal 'For the Defense of Stalingrad.' It is a symbol of our victories on the banks of the great Russian river, the Volga. We have carried this banner through air raids and artillery fire, through the bloodshed and flames of war. It has witnessed our recent victories and a happy event—the linkup of the two fronts, the meeting of the Allies who have so greatly contributed to Victory. Please accept this banner, General. It bears the traces of our corp's heavy fighting throughout the war. We hope it will always remind you of the great victory over Nazism and of our nations' wartime friendship."

The General's stern face betrayed emotion. A faint smile spread across his hard, slightly-forbidding mouth, and a twinkle appeared in his deep-set eyes. He shook my hand with emotion, and was about to say something—but coughed instead. At that moment, the heads of the first reporters who had at last crossed the river appeared above the crest of the hill. Frankly, I was somewhat taken aback by that unexpected, noisy invasion of journalists. However, Konstantin Simonov and Alexander Krivitsky handled the situation with exceptional tact. They too shook hands with their colleagues, patted them on the back, and even managed to interview Gen. Huebner and some of the U.S. reporters. Simonov's swarthy face was flushed with excitement.

At last, we set out for the small, picturesque village of Werdau, located some five kilometers from the crossing where I had met our guests. Although the cooks had received their orders the previous day, I was wondering whether they had managed to prepare everything they were supposed to, for I wanted to make a good impression on the quick-witted reporters whom we had not been expecting. It was indeed good, I thought to myself while sitting next to Gen. Huebner in the car, that I had told them to use all the spare dinner settings.

As it turned out, I had nothing to worry about. As soon as I entered the small garden near the tidy house, I saw a virtual miracle unfold before my eyes on the beckoning lawn beneath the blooming apple trees. Only during dinner could I judge what kind of impression our preparations had made on our American guests. Until then, I was so worried that there wouldn't be enough seats for everyone that while inviting the visitors to the table I wasn't able to concentrate on anything else. Soon, however, I heard that expressive American "Oh!" and admiring exclamations as the famous Ukrainian *borsch* was being served and the guests were tasting their first spoonfuls. Siberian *pelmeni* (dumplings) were served after the first course. In short, as Misha Konovalov assured me, "Everything was tip-top."

About forty of us were sitting together at a table which had been beautifully arranged. The delicious aroma of food expertly prepared mingled with the scent of apple blossoms. The atmosphere was perfectly suited to a friendly, frank discussion, and that's just what we had. We talked about the war—heavy combat and the glorious victories, a soldier's duty and wartime friendship, the perils of Nazism and the necessity of struggling against it. We drank to our victory and the imminent end of the war, to our meeting and the friendship of the Allied armies, to the prosperity of our peoples, to mankind and the happiness of humanity.

The dinner was nearly over when the Americans mentioned our T-34 tank. Praising its performance, they asked us a few technical questions about it. So I offered to show them the tank, and we all set off for the adjoining estate.

I don't mean to put down the foreign journalists who were at the dinner, but I couldn't help noticing their fondness for Russian vodka. This was also true of the U.S. jeep drivers who had brought our guests. Realizing that they might not be in any shape to drive, I ordered our drivers to take the visitors back to the river crossing.

We parted on the best of terms. The Americans got into their cars as they held huge bunches of spring flowers which our men had picked for them in a small field near the village of Werdau.

COL. GEN. GLEB BAKLANOV (1910-1976) was Chief of Staff of an infantry regiment in the early years of the Great Patriotic War. He took part in the Smolensk Offensive, the Battle of Moscow, and commanded a division in the Battle of Stalingrad. In the postwar period, Gen. Baklanov held various prominent posts in the USSR Ministry of Defense, and commanded the troops of the Siberian Military District.

29. VLADIMIR ORLOV

"The soldiers never used big, fancy words—they simply pledged to promote their friendship for one another, and devote the rest of their lives to preventing another war."

(Novosti Press)

As I look back on my life, memories of the hard times of the war years immediately come to mind. Along with the Fifty-eighth Infantry Division—the first to link up with the Americans at the Elbe—I fought all the way from Stalingrad to Prague. I did so first as deputy commander of an independent reconnaissance company, and later as a division staff officer. Although I experienced so much during those four years of active duty, the linkup at the Elbe was quite special because of the joy I felt at meeting the Allies, knowing that victory was finally at hand.

It was such a happy event! Still, I've often had moments of sadness when I've thought of my comrades who didn't live to see that day. I yet remember Capt. Fyodor Popov, my commander and close friend. One of the division's best scouts, he was killed right before my eyes as our patrol was fighting on the Don. From the pocket of his blood-stained tunic, I took the snapshot of a little boy: "To Daddy from his son Vladik. Orsk, February 19, 1942." The words had been written by his wife. So many soldiers like Fyodor Popov fell on the battlefield! They too had made it possible for us to finally reach the Elbe.

(Novosti Press)

American soldiers boarding racing shell to return to Torgau.

News of the April 25 linkup with the Americans flashed through the division. Our division commander, Maj. Gen. Vladimir Rusakov, reported it to Gen. Gleb Baklanov, commander of the Thirty-fourth Infantry Corps. Gen. Rusakov sent a group of officers—myself included—to take part in the official meeting with the U.S. representatives. We were all looking forward to that meeting. Rusakov, realizing that his division was taking part in an historic event, seemed especially excited.

At last, the meeting took place on April 26 at 5:00 P.M. in the town of Werdau, located across from Torgau on the east bank of the Elbe. Twenty-eight officers represented the Americans. We had about as many. One by one, the boats carrying the Americans approached the east bank and were moored to the pier. Maj. Gen. Emil F. Reinhardt, commander of the U.S. Sixty-ninth Infantry Division, walked up to Gen. Rusakov, and the two of them joined in a long, hearty handshake. Recorded by numerous photographers, that handshake became a symbol of the Allies' wartime collaboration.

Maj. Mikhail Zhdanov served as interpreter for their lively

conversation. A few minutes later, Soviet officers accompanied the visitors to an old mansion nearby which housed our division HQ. Although a short walk, it was quite a procession beneath three flags—those of the Soviet Union, the United States, and Great Britain. High-ranking officers of the Sixty-ninth Division walked alongside their Soviet counterparts. Both sides spoke different languages, but it was obvious they had accomplished their task.

Our eyes were riveted on the two division commanders. Although Gen. Reinhardt seemed to be a very reserved person, his attitude toward us was quite friendly. Gen. Rusakov was thirty-five years old at the time. I knew that intelligent, fearless commander very well, because I had carried out his orders on many occasions. Our division's advance to the Elbe had been a most difficult one. On our way there, in heavy combat, thousands of our officers and men had been wounded, including the division commander himself. He had been seriously injured while leading his troops against a Nazi counterattack beyond the Dniester. And so our General was a real soldier.

Accepting an American flag from Gen. Reinhardt, Gen. Rusakov said with emotion that we would be loyal to our friendship, and hoped our descendants would keep it alive. Gen. Reinhardt's gift symbolized the Americans' wartime friendship and alliance with our armed forces, which had borne the brunt of the war.

During those historic days, the contacts between the rank-and-file soldiers of both armies were especially memorable because they were so emotional and friendly. The soldiers never used big, fancy words—they simply pledged to promote their friendship for one another, and devote the rest of their lives to preventing another war. This was especially true of the meetings which took place between our division's 173rd and 175th Regiments and the soldiers of the U.S. 273rd Infantry Regiment.

30. ALEXEI GORLINSKY

"US President Harry S. Truman had instructed the General to decorate us on the occasion of our common victory over Nazism."

By April 23, 1945, the Fifth Guards Army had reached the Elbe near Prettin, Torgau, and Riesa. For several months prior, I'd been the acting Chief of Artillery. Late on April 24, Maj. Gen. Poluyektov, commander of our Army's artillery, assigned me the task of inspecting all divisions of the Thirty-fourth Infantry Corps to determine the potential use of artillery pieces in sectors where it was anticipated there would be combat. I was to leave at once.

By dawn of the 25th, I had already reached the 118th Division on our right flank and determined that the division was not actively engaged in combat. This meant that if necessary, I could transfer some of its artillery to areas occupied by other divisions of the corps. I then left for the Fifty-eighth Infantry Division, which was located at the center of the corps' combat formation.

The weather was good, the visibility excellent. I heard our artillery fire several kilometers south of Torgau. Obviously, we were firing just to harass the enemy, rather than to hit any specific targets. I carefully inspected the terrain just ahead of me, and saw several Soviet soldiers approaching a bridge. One of them took out a flare-gun and shot a red flare. I knew that if the Americans were on the opposite bank, they would reply with a green flare, but this didn't occur. The Soviet soldiers came to a halt, fired several times into the air, and waited for a response. Someone then began shouting from the opposite bank, but the words were indistinguishable. Later, Second Lt. William Robertson, commander of the American reconnaissance patrol, told us that they simply hadn't had a green flare with them because they hadn't expected to meet us.

The Americans crossed to our side of the river the following day—April 26. The most impatient and agile of them climbed across the blown road bridge. Others came over in boats which seemed to appear from out of nowhere, their oarsmen rowing very strenuously. We hugged each other, shouted *"Hitler kaput!"*, and exchanged simple war mementoes. Within minutes, many men had cut off the buttons of their tunics and army coats, and removed the stars from their caps. The Americans were fascinated by our Guards insignia. Army capes were quickly spread out over the ground and were soon laden with canned food, bread, vodka, and whiskey. We drank to our meeting, to peace and friendship.

During the latter part of May, a group of generals and officers of the Fifth Guards Army—myself included—went to Leipzig, then part of the U.S. occupation zone. There, Gen. Hodges, commander of the U.S. First Army, awarded us American military decorations on behalf of President Truman on the occasion of our common victory over Nazism.

MAJ. GEN. ALEXEI GORLINSKY was born in 1918 in Kiev. He graduated with a degree in Chemistry from the University of Kiev in 1941. During the Great Patriotic War, Gorlinsky was a front-line artillery officer. He was wounded and shell-shocked. After the war, he served as a lecturer at the Military Academy of the General Staff. He is now retired, and is an Honorary Citizen of Dallas, Texas, and the state of Kansas.

(Novosti Press)

31. IVAN KONYEV

*"The horse I gave Bradley was a handsome and
well-trained Don stallion."*

April 25 was a day of important events. The most
important did not occur, however, in Berlin, but on
the Elbe, when Gen. Gleb Baklanov's Thirty-
fourth Guards Corps of Gen. Alexei Zhadov's
Fifth Guards Army linked up with American troops. It was there, in
the heart of Germany, that Hitler's army was finally cut in two.

Units of the German Ninth and Twelfth Armies, as well as of the
Third Panzer Army, were in and near Berlin. Some were north of the
city. To the south was the entire Army Group Center under the
command of Field Marshal Schörner.

The two Allied Armies, unimpeded by the enemy, met in an
atmosphere of calm. It had finally taken place after many years of

fighting, of numerous military operations and battles. The following is an excerpt from the report we sent GHQ:

> At 13.30 hours on April 25, 1945, units of the 175th Infantry Regiment of the 58th Guards Division met a reconnaissance group of 69th Infantry Division of the 5th Army Corps of the American 1st Army in the advance zone of the 5th Guards Army, in the area of Strehla on the Elbe.
>
> On the same day, the advance battalion of the 173rd Guards Infantry Regiment of the same 58th Guards division met another reconnaissance group of the 69th Infantry Division of the 5th Army Corps of the American 1st Army in the area of Torgau on the Elbe.

I first met Gen. Omar N. Bradley, Commander of the American Twelfth Army Group, a week after the linkup of Soviet and American troops on the Elbe. Our meeting took place at my Command Post some forty kilometers northeast of Torgau. Bradley arrived with a retinue of generals and officers and a large number of reporters and newspaper photographers—too many of them, I thought at the time. Besides myself, members of the Military Council of the Front were present—Alexei Zhadov, Commander of the Fifth Guards Army, and Gleb Baklanov, Commander of the Thirty-fourth Guards Infantry Corps. Their troops had been the first to meet the Americans at the Elbe. We were also accompanied by representatives of the press, photographers, and cameramen, but considerably fewer than those with the Americans.

There have been many fluctuations in Soviet-American relations. Although the Soviet side has done everything it could so that it would be otherwise, even today our relations leave much to be desired. But on that day—May 5, 1945—the meeting between Bradley and myself was, I must say, straightforward and candid. We were soldiers, not diplomats. This was evident in both meetings, which were official yet friendly.

The General and I examined his map which showed the positions of the American troops on that day—May 5. Bradley briefly explained which of his units had reached the agreed-upon line of contact with us, and when they had linked up. He then asked me about our plans for taking Prague, and whether the Americans could be of any help. His question did not surprise me. Although Soviet troops had not as yet gone on the offensive against Schörner's group, the Americans realized that we would be launching one in the immediate future.

I told Bradley we didn't need any help, that an advance of American troops farther east of the established line of demarcation would only complicate matters and confuse our troops, which we did not desire. I therefore asked him not to undertake what he proposed. Bradley agreed, and said that the troops under his command would remain at the established line of contact.

During the dinner which followed my meeting with Bradley, I made my first toast, noting the trials and tribulations the Soviet Army had endured on its way to victory. I spoke of the important role President Roosevelt had played in forging the anti-Hitler coalition and in all subsequent events. I had been genuinely, deeply moved by Roosevelt's death. It was still fresh in my memory. In my official condolences on the U.S. President's untimely death, I expressed my personal feelings and the hope that the new President would continue Roosevelt's policies. Unfortunately, this hope was not realized. Roosevelt's successor very soon helped to aggravate Soviet-U.S. relations. Talking of our common struggle against the Nazi invaders, I spoke of the indisputable merits of the officers and men of the U.S. Twelfth Army Group.

In reply, Gen. Bradley toasted the courage of the Soviet soldiers and the valor of the troops of the first Ukrainian Front. He said they had served as examples for the American generals, officers, and men. Dwelling on Roosevelt's contribution, he regretted that the President had not lived to see the happy day of victory. He then toasted our meeting.

The first official toasts were followed by a friendly conversation interrupted now and then by "local toasts"—as I called them—to representatives of our respective staffs, to army commanders and members of various armed services.

The toasts were cordial, sincere, and showed that we truly respected each other and appreciated this wartime friendship which had been born of our struggle against a common enemy. After dinner, I invited Bradley and his companions to a concert given by the Song and Dance Company of the First Ukrainian Front. Organized in 1943 in Kiev by Lidya Chernyshova, this Company—with its excellent singers, musicians, and dancers—was extremely popular at the Front. When the Company sang America's national anthem, the Americans in the auditorium joined in and enthusiastically applauded when it ended. They also applauded when the Company sang the national anthem of the Soviet Union.

The Company outdid itself that day. In addition to Soviet songs, they performed "There's a Tavern in the Town"—an American song—and the British song "It's a Long Way to Tipperary." The guests were especially delighted with the best part of the Company's repertory, Ukrainian and Russian folk dances. These dances usually make an unforgettable impression, but when added to the audience's already festive mood and high spirits, they were even more effective.

Gen. Bradley, who was sitting next to me, asked numerous questions about the Company. He wanted to know how the performers had ended up at the Front. I thought he didn't quite believe me when I told him that the Company consisted of servicemen who had fought with troops at the Front. But I was telling the truth—most of the performers really had enlisted as rank-and-file soldiers. Later, when the Company gained official status, the members performed for the forward-echelon troops, often dangerously close to the front lines.

Thanking me for the concert, Bradley announced that the U.S. government had decided to decorate me, as Commander of the First Ukrainian Front, with the highest American decoration. He then presented it to me with warm congratulations. My comrades in arms who were there with me were equally honored by my award, for they regarded it as a sign that our ally appreciated the contribution the First Ukrainian Front had made to the fighting.

After the ceremony, Bradley and I left the mansion where I had received the award. In the presence of a large audience which had gathered on the occasion of Bradley's visit, I presented him—on behalf of the First Ukrainian Front troops, and as a symbol of our friendship—with a red banner. I knew he was also going to give me a special gift marking the occasion—a jeep flown in directly from his HQ. I had also made arrangements to present the General with a personal gift—the horse that had been with me everywhere since the summer of 1943, when I had assumed command of the Steppe Front. The horse I gave Bradley was a handsome and well-trained Don stallion—fully out-fitted. Bradley seemed quite pleased with the gift. The jeep he gave me was inscribed with the words, "To the Commander of the 1st Ukrainian Army Group from the soldiers of the American 12th Army Group." He also gave me a U.S. flag and an American submachine gun.

A few days later, I returned Gen. Bradley's visit.

We drove in our own cars as far as Torgau, where we were met by a senior officer and interpreters who accompanied us to Leipzig. Bradley expected me in Leipzig, and offered to fly me to his HQ in Wiesbaden in his personal airplane—Wiesbaden was quite a distance from Leipzig. We boarded his SI-47 and were escorted by two fighter squadrons all the way to the HQ. The pilots demonstrated first-class flying skills as they continuously changed formation. When our plane landed near Kassel, the squadrons spectacularly departed, flying at various altitudes, some of which were quite low. It then occurred to me that the escort was not only meant to be an honor guard, but also to demonstrate flying skills.

On our way from the airfield near Kassel, we were accompanied by a motorized escort consisting of several armored cars driving in front, a car with a loud siren, and then the car with Bradley, myself, and the interpreter. Bringing up the rear were a few armored personnel carriers and three tanks. Troops representing all U.S. armed services, with the possible exception of the Navy, were lined up at intervals along our entire route.

Numerous staff officers and an even larger crowd of news correspondents had gathered near the building we drove up to. In the building's main hall, Bradley suggested we have cocktails, and told us that they were made according to his own recipe. The drinks were ladled out of a huge copper kettle into army mugs, which they told us was a tradition. Well, traditions had to be respected . . .

After we finished our drinks, Bradley took me to his headquarters at the other end of the city. An honor guard, again consisting of all armed services, had lined up in front of the building. We inspected the honor guard, and I greeted them. Then I asked the General to order them to stand at attention. After he had done so, I decorated Gen. Bradley on behalf of the Soviet government with the Order of Suvorov, First Class. Reserved as he was, he was visibly moved. We embraced as friends, and I congratulated him.

We went inside and were ushered into a hall where tables had been set for dinner. This time, too, the dinner began with toasting. The first was proposed by the host. I returned it, and toasted Bradley, his friends, and comrades in arms seated at the table.

The dinner conversation hardly touched on the war. Suvorov was the only military topic we discussed. Now that Bradley had been decorated with the Order of Suvorov, he was very interested in hearing about the great man, whom he apparently had never heard of before. I told Bradley that Suvorov was the best Russian military leader in our history, and that the Order of Suvorov was primarily presented to high-ranking officers. It was considered the top decoration for army commanders in charge of large military units. With great sincerity, I added that Marshal Stalin had personally asked me to present this decoration to Gen. Bradley.

After dinner, two violinists in army uniform—one older than the other—performed several magnificent duets for us. No wonder the music was so beautifully played—the violinists were none other than the famous Jascha Heifetz and his son. In between selections, Bradley looked at me with a twinkle in his eye. Clearly, not having believed me when I told him that our Song and Dance Company was comprised of men from the First Ukrainian Front, he had decided to play a joke on me by passing off Jascha Heifetz and his son as soldiers.

I was pleased that Bradley always spoke highly of the Soviet people and their army, and had a high opinion—with what appeared to be genuine satisfaction—of our recent military operations. He demonstrated that he understood all the problems facing the Soviet Army in the fight against Nazi Germany. He told me quite frankly that he believed the Soviet Army had borne the brunt of the war. In other words, he stated what other Western generals—our former allies—later tried to ignore or even deny. We also shared a similar view of the enemy. He considered the German army to be strong, hardened, and capable of fighting stubbornly, expertly, and steadfastly.

The atmosphere of our meeting was informal and relaxed throughout. Our countries were on very good terms then. I left Bradley's HQ in the best of spirits.

IVAN KONYEV (1897-1973), named a Marshal of the Soviet Union in 1944, was twice awarded the title of Hero of the Soviet Union—the Soviet equivalent of the American Congressional Medal of Honor. During the Russian Civil War, he was political commissar of a division and then a corps. During the Great Patriotic War, Konyev was both an army and Front commander. After the war, he held a number of prominent military positions in the Armed Forces of the USSR.

32. Yuri Timoshenko and Yefim Berezin (actors)

"Don't sit under the apple tree with anyone else but me."

The war was over—we could sense this at the headquarters of the army commanded by V.I. Chuikov, who later became a Marshal of the Soviet Union. We had arrived at the HQ to celebrate the great victory over Nazi Germany. On May 9—during the Victory salute—we also fired into the still sky along with the heroic soldiers who had stormed Berlin. Peace at last!

Not long after that, we gave a special performance on the other side of the Elbe for our American allies. That concert had quite a history.

Our choirmaster, Y.P. Sheinin, wanted to impress the Americans with our exquisite, elaborate singing technique. The vehicle he selected for this was a simple American song entitled "Don't Sit Under the Apple Tree."

"I want this song to sound as if it were fine lacework woven by human voices," the choirmaster enthusiastically told us. It took us quite a while to choose the best key, and the arrangement of the song was changed three times. We rehearsed day and night until we got sick and tired of it.

One day when the choir—enraged—was about to tear the conductor to shreds, all of us received orders to stop rehearsing and get ready to leave in an hour for the American positions. We were to go in full dress but without weapons.

We reached the blown bridge spanning the Elbe where an American barge was waiting for us. We left our buses and gathered around an American soldier who was standing near the crossing chewing gum and smiling amicably. At last, we had a chance to try out our English, and we asked him a number of "highly intelligent questions" such as "How do you do?", "How old are you?", and "What time is it?" Considering that we added "mister" to all of them, they didn't come out too bad.

The soldier—using many words we didn't know—answered at length. We nodded vigorously and smiled at him all the same. He also tried to ask us questions, but we interrupted him with more of our "clever" questions. After we'd completely exhausted our knowledge of English, we noticed the word "Krovchak" written on his helmet, and wondered what it meant.

"That's my last name," he replied.

"But it's a Ukrainian name, isn't it? Are you Ukrainian?"

"Sure," he replied in Ukrainian. "My name's Fedko Krovchak . . ."

We roared with laughter. It was so funny to hear a native speaker of English using an extremely provincial Ukrainian dialect spoken only in remote Carpathian villages.

He told us his father, born in the Ukrainian city of Ternopol, had emigrated to America before World War I. His father had done his best to preserve the Ukrainian language in the family. The children were not allowed to speak English at home. The Krovchaks were living in New York, but the mother still cooked *borsch, galuski, varenki,* and garlic rolls for dinner. He told us that men of Slavic descent from all nearby U.S. detachments had been sent out to meet us and serve as interpreters.

A huge barn had been converted into a theater especially for our performance. It was packed to capacity, and a crowd had gathered at the entrance. The U.S. soldiers cheered us cordially and looked us over with obvious curiosity. As soon as the generals arrived, the company was invited onto the stage.

The concert began with both national anthems. Before coming out onto the stage, we spent our time in the wings watching the audience—at least 1,500 men. They were all chewing gum, jaws moving rhythmically. Each time a singer would hit a high note or a dancer perform a complicated trick, the moving jaws would all stop—as if on command. Each song and dance was greeted by a burst of deafening whistling (which we were not used to), cheering, and applause. The audience asked for encores for most of the acts. We too had prepared an interlude in English, which was a great success.

At last, someone announced the American song we were going

to sing. Waiting for total silence, the conductor came up to the bass section and whispered, "Don't forget about the legato in the second line of the third couplet." He then approached the trombone players and reminded them to make the first note of the second line as soft as possible. Finally, he raised his hands, and the band began playing the introduction.

The members of the audience, who had been holding their breath in anticipation, sighed in appreciation and started nodding their heads to the beat of the music. Then the choir stepped in and performed a septaphonic chord. Hardly had they sung two bars than the entire audience joined in and carried on in hoarse, throaty voices . . .

The conductor turned to stone. He stopped conducting, but the song went on. All the spectators, including the generals, were beating time and shouting as loud as they could:

> Don't sit under the apple tree
> With anyone else but me,
> Anyone else but me,
> Anyone else but me—
> Till I come marching home . . .

The Russian choir and its American listeners, neglecting all the subtleties that had been worked out by the conscientious conductor, roared together in two languages. The chorus was so powerful that we may have lifted the ceiling with the sound of our triumphant voices.

The singers and musicians were in stitches. Trumpet and trombone players were playing out of tune because their mouths wouldn't obey them. Accordion players bit their lips to suppress laughter, but the tears rolling down their cheeks gave them away. The choir, still singing, simply groaned with laughter.

When the song had come to an end, the highest ranking general present ran up to the stage and requested an encore. He also asked the conductor to face the audience so that everyone could join in.

The conductor had to oblige.

After the performance, the same general thanked us for the pleasure we'd given everyone, and invited us all to a banquet. The banquet was unusual. It seems that the commanders of the various units we'd performed for couldn't agree on who would be host. As a result, each unit expected some of us for dinner. So as not to offend them, we had to break up into groups of three or four and go to different parties.

Waiting for us in the street was a whole row of jeeps. Our group was accompanied by an American soldier of Polish extraction. He introduced himself and assured us—in Polish—of the cordial friendship on the part of all the American soldiers. As we were driving away, a stranger in a U.S. Army uniform jumped into our car. After a brief exchange of words, our Polish-American told the driver to stop and ordered the stranger out of the car. The man refused. The driver, who was a very big man, then pushed the Polish-American out of the car. Right then, an officer rushed up and ordered the stranger be let in.

"This is a security man," the Polish-American whispered to us, and cursed loudly.

On our way to the party, our escort was clearly angry. He calmed down only when we arrived.

At the entrance of the mess hall, we were greeted by a ruddy-cheeked chef wearing a snow-white cap. He presented each of us with a bunch of flowers, swung the doors open, and ushered us in. After we'd been seated at the festively-laden table, our hosts switched off the electric lights and lit candles. Our Polish interpreter explained that this was done to create an informal, gay atmosphere. After a short time, he rose and said loudly, "Quiet, please! I have a toast to make!"

He asked all us Soviet guests to stand, and said as he pointed to the medal "For the Defense of Stalingrad," "All Americans, French, and British should worship every Russian decorated with this medal!"

The party burst with applause, cheers, and hurrahs.

The silence which fell as usual after the first toast was broken by the security man. His face was crimson, he was coughing loudly, and had to spit several times. It turned out that someone had poured vinegar into his glass. We later found out that that someone had been our driver. He kept harassing the security man throughout the party. During the second toast, he quietly pulled back the man's chair, which ended up with the security man sitting hard on the floor. Then the driver took a candle from the table and attempted to light the man's cap that was hanging from the back of his chair.

Among us was a man from our orchestra who played the

trumpet. His name was Nikolai Rudy. ("Rudy" in Ukrainian means "redhead.") He called himself Niko Rudol and ignored anyone who addressed him as Rudy. He was a jazz fan. When the party was in full swing, he admitted he had his trumpet with him, and wanted to play for the American jazz fans. Everyone welcomed his idea with enthusiasm. One of those present turned out to be an excellent pianist.

Timoshenko and our Polish interpreter, acting as the MCs, announced that Niko Rudol would perform an improvisation of a tune from the then-popular American movie "Sun Valley Serenade." The piano and trumpet started playing the familiar tune. Then the pianist, as if challenging the trumpeter, stepped up the tempo and played a variation rather close to the main theme.

That was the signal for the trumpeter to step in. Niko, obviously excited, raised the trumpet to his lips and began his improvisation. His trumpet croaked, bleated, roared, screeched, and wept. It ended on such a high note that the Americans burst into a storm of applause and cheers before he'd even finished. Some of them picked up Niko and began tossing him into the air.

Everyone was just convinced that Rudol must be one of the best jazz trumpeters in Russia. But Niko said, "Well, I'm the second-best trumpeter in the city of Vinnitsa. It's too bad you can't hear our best man."

The Americans, amazed that this unknown city had such a superb jazz tradition, were eager to hear more about Vinnitsa.

(*Novosti Press*)

33. SERGEI KRUSHINSKY

"People will later argue if April 25 had been sunny or cloudy, if there had been a strong wind or not."

From Pravda, *April 28, 1945*

Not so long ago, hardly anyone had heard of the German town of Torgau on the Elbe. Certainly very few of us could say we'd ever known of it. It was only on April 25, 1945, that the town became historically significant. At 13:30 hours, troops of the First Ukrainian Front coming from the east and the Allied Anglo-American armies approaching from the west linked up near Torgau, in the very heart of Germany, thereby cutting the front in two. This means that Nazi troops fighting in Northern Germany have been cut off from their forces in the south . . .

I landed at the Elbe in the morning. It took our plane slightly more than an hour to cross the territory that had been occupied by Soviet troops during the April offensive. We flew over the Neisse and Spree, over a vast wooded area with villages and towns scattered here and there. Everywhere, we noticed fresh traces of our bold offensive and the powerful shelling by our artillery. The edges of the woods were lined with enemy trenches, the clearings pockmarked with foxholes. The streets of the towns and villages were barricaded.

Smashed guns and burned-out tanks had been abandoned everywhere along the enemy's line of defense. The roads were filled with the remnants of army transports. It was mute testimony to what had befallen the Nazis in the wide strip of land between the Spree and Elbe. The farther west we went, the more striking was the picture of Nazi Germany's defeat. Our firepower had swept away, routed everything in its path . . .

Hitler's Germany is collapsing. The local *führers* have given up all hope of evacuating because they have nowhere to go. The *Volkssturmers*, when taken prisoner, are found to have civilian clothes in their packs—they are quite prepared to "change." As our troops have seized areas along the Elbe, they've seen crowds of refugees fleeing from east to west. The refugees have become totally confused, forced to halt because they have nowhere to retreat to...

It's difficult to comprehend the larger significance of recent events. No wonder—every detail might prove to be historically important. People will later argue if April 25 had been sunny or cloudy, if there had been a strong wind or not. But today, intoxicated by their victories, our soldiers scarcely know if it is day or night...

Now they are in the very heart of Germany, on the Elbe. My plane is flying through the hot smoke that blankets the burning woods. The greenish-gray spots on the roads are, in fact, groups of prisoners on the march. Overtaking them are the multicolored lines of Germany's liberated prisoners. They stop and wave at us until our plane disappears from sight. Our pilot, Senior Lt. Syomin, responds by slightly tilting the wing. However, his eyes are constantly scanning the sky and the land ahead, because isolated groups of enemy submachine gunners are still roaming the woods, and Nazi fighter planes—alone or in twos—are still lurking in the sky...

Finally, we could see the Elbe slowly flowing between low banks as it made its way down a broad plain. Casting one or more glances at it, Syomin wrote in large letters across a sheet of paper: "The last line!" We were totally baffled by what we saw next. Lining the banks of the Elbe were silent guns, machine guns, and other weapons. Front-line soldiers were walking freely amid trenches. It looked so strange that we thought we were in a dream.

The plane landed alongside the Elbe. The officers and men had already washed their dusty, sooty hands in the river water. They were happily smiling, excited by such an extraordinary event. Having cleaned their weapons, they had begun to tend to themselves—they shaved, wrote letters home, and enjoyed the opportunity to do so in safety. How wonderful it must have been for them!

We were told at the Command Post that the first unofficial meetings between Soviet and American reconnaissance men had taken place in the morning on the west bank of the Elbe. A group of Americans had reached the east bank in a ferry later that morning. A Soviet company commander, Senior Lt. Goloborodko, had shaken hands with Lt. Kotzebue, commander of a U.S. reconnaissance patrol.

The sector in which the Allies linked up presented quite an interesting sight. In the town of Riesa, we examined the blown bridges. The enemy had blown the railway bridge in only one place—near the west bank. The road bridge had been completely destroyed. This had been a useless exercise, however, because the Allied armies had approached the river from both sides—east and west.

Trains packed with refugees had been halted at the approaches to the Elbe. This is the end of the territory chosen by the Nazis for "the reduction of the Front." Indeed, the Front had been reduced to an absolute minimum, vanishing entirely.

In the evening, our plane took off again, making a farewell circle over the Elbe. We headed eastward. Although silence has fallen on the scene of the Allies' linkup, fighting is still underway farther north, farther south. The sky is filled with smoke and dust. The indefatigable Soviet artillery keeps up its firing. Tanks driven by experienced hands are forcing their way forward, kilometer by kilometer.

Our gallant infantry is pressing onward, inspired by one idea— to finish the enemy off.

Nothing can stop this drive. The power accumulated by the Soviet people will rout the last centers of resistance put up by the Nazis, who dared raise the sword against our country four years ago.

SOVIET JOURNALIST SERGEI KRUSHINSKY (1909-1959) was *Pravda's* special correspondent during the war.

34. KONSTANTIN SIMONOV

"Everyone is weeping."

The meeting of Soviet and American soldiers, as everyone now knows, took place on April 25, 1945, at the Elbe, not far from Torgau.

Krasnaya zvezda[1] correspondent Sasha Krivitsky and I were there at that meeting and at two others which occurred days later. Photographs taken then of us standing with Soviet and American soldiers at the Elbe still remain. They're still there in a desk drawer full of mementos of that time—nickel-plated American insignia which had been traded for officer stars taken from epaulets. Still there is the draft of a brief news story which had been sent to *Krasnaya zvezda* from somewhere south of Torgau. In it are the names of the commanders of the first divisions which linked up—the American Gen. Reinhardt, and our Gen. Rusakov. Names of the commanders of the American patrol and of our own are there—Lt. Robertson and Lt. Silvashko—the men who first met at the Elbe, where at long last not a single Nazi soldier remained between the Americans and us.

In my memories, there is still a measure of that joy we felt then, a joy so great and which at the time was not yet weighed down by any future doubts or apprehensions.

So much remains in my memories. Yet in the notebooks left over from those days, there's nothing about all of this, as if it were a total blank!

I remember the POW camp south of Leipzig where our own soldiers had been imprisoned, which was being guarded by the Americans. An American colonel—an intelligence officer—drove us there. Incidentally, he didn't even attempt to conceal from us what his military duties were.

I remember the camp more clearly than anything else. But in this instance, a short article comes to my aid. It appeared in *Komsomolskaya pravda* in late 1945:

". . . We are entering the gates. The first person to meet us is a pale girl who looks at us attentively, without any particular joy.

"Are you a Russian girl?' I ask.

"Russian,' she says, looking at us in even greater bewilderment.

"And only right then do I grasp that our new uniforms with their epaulets have forced her to mistake us for someone else.

"We take several steps. Someone darts toward us, runs up, and shouts:

"They're ours! They're ours!' and turning abruptly, races into one of the barracks.

"We walk through the camp. More and more people gather all around us. And by the time we approach the center of a square enclosed by barbed wire, we're surrounded by a crowd of thousands.

"I walk up onto the steps of a platform. Overcome by emotion, I stumble. My legs are shaking. I'm almost afraid of falling. Now I'm being asked to say the first words in this camp, words which have come from the Motherland, words which those here have not heard—some for a year, others for two, yet others for three, almost four.

"My throat is dry. I don't have the strength to say even a word. I slowly gaze out at the immense ocean of people crowding around me.

"I've already been told this was a punitive camp, that its inmates were prisoners of war being punished for bad behavior, forced laborers who had refused to work.

"What suffering was written on the faces of these people, even if you could read only a tenth of what they had endured.

"I began to speak, yet I myself don't know what I'm saying. I didn't remember then, and don't remember now.

"Then I come down from the steps, and someone else gets up. It's the officer who came with me. He also says something, quite likely, the same thing I'd said.

"I can't make out his words, yet I'm overwhelmed with a feeling of frenzied joy over this meeting. And I began to weep and, having wept a little, look up for the first time and see that everyone too is weeping.

"And then they walk with us. We walk together with this crowd of thousands through the entire camp.

"There beside me, stretching his instrument to both sides, is an accordion player with tightly-pressed lips. All his teeth have been knocked out and he speaks like an old man. For this reason he'd rather play than talk . . ."

Perhaps now my writing would be better than what I wrote in that newspaper article. Yet I cherish it because it was written almost at the very end of the war. And I have no desire to replace words I wrote then with those written thirty years later.

I would want to add only two details which weren't mentioned in the article, but which remain in my memory alone. I not only spoke to the camp inmates, but also recited "Wait for me."[2] And among those who wept was that same American colonel who had brought us to this camp.

KONSTANTIN MIKHAILOVICH SIMONOV (1915E1979) was a prominent Soviet writer and poet. He was awarded the Lenin Prize for his trilogy *The Living and the Dead*.

1. *Krasnaya zvezda* was and still is the newspaper of the Soviet Armed Forces. During World War II, it was the Soviet equivalent of *Yank* and *Stars and Stripes*.
2. Simonov's "Wait for Me," written in 1941, was the best known war poem in the USSR. Most Soviet soldiers knew it by heart:

Wait for me, I shall return,
Only wait for me,
Wait for me, when you will learn
How sad life can be,
Wait, when all the snows are gone,
Wait, through summer's spell,
Wait, when friends who waited long
Forget friends so well.
Wait, when letters coming late
No more wait for you.
Wait, when those like us who wait
Tire of waiting too.

Wait for me, I shall return,
Wish them not good will,
It is time for them to spurn
All they know so well.
Let the mother and the son
Think that I am dead,
Let all my friends one by one
Cease to wait instead.
Let them drink the bitter wine,

Tribute to my soul . . .
Wait. Rush not with friends of mine,
All who drink their fill.

Wait for me, I shall return,
To spite all the deaths.
Those surprised will say in turn,
'Luckier than the rest.'
Those surprised won't comprehend
How in all the mire,
Your own waiting without end
Saved me from the Fire.
How I survived, tempting fate,
We know both of us—
You alone knew how to wait,
Like nobody else.

III: Forty Years After

Torgau, April 25, 1985. (*ADN-Zentralbild*)

INTRODUCTION

Joseph Polowsky remained loyal to the Oath of the Elbe in death as in life. After learning in 1983 that he had terminal cancer, Joe resolved to be buried in Torgau, where the Robertson Patrol had linked up with Soviet troops on April 25, 1945. His burial there at a time of heightened U.S.-Soviet tensions would, he believed, symbolize "one of the few remaining ties between the two countries." He explained, "My view is that my burial at Torgau was paid for with the spilling of the blood of the soldiers of the World War II allies of the East and West."

But Joe had neither the money nor East German clearance to be buried in Torgau. What's more, the prospects for immediate help were bleak. Yet he was certain in a religious sort of way that it would all come to pass. If his body was not sent to Torgau within eleven days of his death, he stipulated, "I am to be buried with a minimum of ceremony in a simple Christian Protestant service in a cemetery in West Berlin, with no headstone over my grave—my body to remain there until some future time when clearance is granted, at which time my body is to be disinterred and transferred to Torgau."

Time was short. In the months just preceding his death, Joe took the unusual step of meeting with his mortician on a regular basis to discuss the details of the funeral. He frantically appealed to friends and strangers alike for burial funds. Some money did come in, from people such as author Studs Terkel. But it wasn't enough. Joe petitioned the East German government for permission to be buried in Torgau. No reply. All the while, he continued to urge everyone he met to take the Oath of the Elbe. Little interest. "I'm out of sync with the times," he said."I'm pretty much of a nonperson."

Finally, on the night of October 17, 1983, Joe died in a Chicago veterans hospital.

Now what?

Within days of the death, the East German government granted Joe's request to be buried in Torgau. Close friend LeRoy Wolins—bookseller and Vice Commander of Veterans for Peace—went deeply in debt to make up the transportation costs of the burial.

And so on November 26, 1983, Pvt. Joe Polowsky was buried—in a cold Torgau rain. "My life has been a lifelong love affair with the Stars and Stripes," he once said. "My coffin will be draped with the American flag. I believe I have served the United States faithfully and well in war and in peace."

Both American and Soviet World War II veterans bore the flag-draped casket to the grave. Said Soviet Elbe veteran Maj. Gen. Alexei Gorlinsky, "We affirm our allegiance to the Spirit of the Elbe." Standing at the gravesite, the Rev. William Sloane Coffin read from the Book of Micah:

> And it shall come to pass in the better days that the mountain of the house of the Lord shall be raised above all mountains, and nations shall come and beat their swords into plowshares and their spears into pruning hooks. And nation shall not lift up sword against nation.

Joe Polowsky was laid to rest. His dream went with him. Or did it?

Three Americans at the burial cooperated the following year to return to Torgau for a fortieth anniversary observance of the Meeting at the Elbe. They were LeRoy Wolins; William R. Beswick, Vice President of the Fighting Sixty-ninth Infantry Division Association; and Robert Swan, Jr., a Kansas insurance agent and peace activist of many years. Beswick—a pallbearer at the Polowsky funeral—devoted more than a year to organizing a delegation of 115 American veterans and their wives for the Torgau celebrations. Wolins, the major organizer of the Polowsky funeral, worked with Swan and media consultant Mark Scott to form a "Fortieth Anniversary Journey for Peace" comprised of fifty Americans from twenty states who would "link up" in Torgau with Beswick's group as well as with Soviets and East Germans. Meanwhile, the influential Soviet War Veterans Committee and the Peace Council of the German Democratic Republic were enlisting their own members for the celebrations with the Americans.

On April 25, 1985—forty years after the Meeting at the Elbe and more than one and a half years after the burial of Joe Polowsky—some three hundred American and Soviet citizens, led by their Elbe veterans, met in Torgau to celebrate the first linkup. Soviet Gen. Yuri Naumenko read greetings to those present from General Secretary Mikhail Gorbachev. Swan read messages which Scott had received from former Presidents Richard Nixon and Jimmy Carter. The Hon. Horst Sindermann, President of the East German parliament, personally addressed the audience.

It was a Great Event, perhaps the greatest people-to-people

event in U.S.-Soviet relations since the first Meeting at the Elbe, when countless ordinary people had spontaneously joined in a celebration of life amid the fresh scent of lilacs. On that April day in 1985, more than 25,000 smiling human beings from many nations crowded the narrow streets of the small town of Torgau on the Elbe. Almost five hundred news correspondents reported on this second linkup to an estimated one billion people in more than sixty countries.

Joe Polowsky could—for the moment—rest in peace.

35. MURRY SCHULMAN

"We struck it rich."

The names of the American Elbe veterans who went to Russia in 1955? Well, in addition to myself, there was Elijah Sams from North Carolina. Charles Forrester from South Carolina. Then there was Fred Johnston from Pennsylvania, Bob Haag from Indiana, Byron Shiver from Florida, Claude Moore from Tennessee, Edwin Jeary from Michigan, and Joe Polowsky from Chicago. All in all, there were nine in our group.

In the early part of 1955, Joe Polowsky sent an invite to the Russians to come to Washington to celebrate the tenth anniversary of the Elbe linkup with American vets. The Russians accepted Joe's invite. Upon making application to come to the United States, however, they found out that they had to be fingerprinted. Now, to my understanding, in Russia only criminals are fingerprinted. They refused to be fingerprinted. So they, in turn, extended an invite to Joe to come with American Elbe vets to take part in the Victory Day celebrations in Moscow.

In late April of 1955, a group of about twelve of us met in Washington to celebrate the tenth anniversary together. While we were there, we were invited to the Soviet Embassy for cocktails. Ambassador Zarubin, as well as the press, were in attendance at this affair. The Russians offered to pay for the whole trip—ten days in the Soviet Union. But this didn't sit right with the group of Americans. We wanted some American sponsor to foot at least half the expense. At that time, though, nobody came forward.

Most of us didn't have much money at the time. Some of the boys had even had to hitchhike to Washington for the small tenth anniversary celebration we had there on April 25. Joe Polowsky came up with about a third of the money the group needed to get to Paris—the Soviets would pick us up there.

Well, the group of nine of us got as far as Idlewild Airport in New York. This was on May 3. We had our passports and visas—but not enough money. We appeared at a televised news conference right there at the airport. Joe said, "God willing, we will raise the $5,580 and go to our mission and accomplish it and present the American point of view to the Soviet people and make a contribution to peace."

As there was no one to pay for the American part of the trip, though, we returned to my home. There we decided we could not accept the Soviet offer—for obvious reasons. We sat around talking that evening. Everybody was going to go home the next day because there was no money in sight.

Then at about twelve midnight, I received a telephone call from Mr. Bernard Barb, a reporter with the *Long Island Press*. After I explained our situation to him, he called Mr. Walt Framer, producer of the TV game show "Strike It Rich" ("The Show with a Heart"). The show was well-known for raising money for worthy causes. Mr. Barb called me back and said we had an invite to appear on "Strike It Rich"—the next morning.

We appeared on the program along with a woman who had two small children and another woman. The woman with the children needed money for the gas and electric bill. The other woman needed a new sewing machine in order to make a living. All we needed was nine plane tickets to Paris and back.

We were the last ones on the program that morning. Mr. Hull asked us questions about our proposed trip and our need for money. After telling everyone why we wanted to go to Russia, he began asking us our questions. The first one dealt with Army or Navy personnel. "Was Harry Arnold an Army or Navy man?" We didn't have any problem with that one. Army, of course. That question was worth $60. In addition, each of us received a box of FAB.(1) Time then ran out. We had to come back the next day to answer the remaining questions.

Before we went on the show again the following morning, Mr. Framer talked to us. He said we had been all right the day before, but suggested that we be a little more enthusiastic, really make a plea to the American people. We were talking about a lot of money, and had a selling job to do.

When the program started this time, we were the first ones on. Besides us was Booker T. Washington's daughter, who was trying to raise funds for a school. Another participant was a handicapped woman who wanted—and got—a typewriter to help her earn a living.

Once again, we explained to the audience what we needed. We began the question period with our previous earnings of $60. Elijah Sams said that if we did not receive enough money for the trip, we would give any money we did receive to the Heart Fund.

We identified the song "Buttons and Bows." This brought us up to $120. The answer to the next question was "Senator Kefauver." We now had $240. Claude Moore—from Newbern, Tennessee—answered the last question with a loud "Tennessee!" We were now up to $500. Mr. Framer then announced to the audience that "Strike It Rich" would match the $500 from our "Heart Fund." Suddenly, we had $1,000, plus a large box of FAB each. I still wanted the American people to foot at least half the cost of our trip to Russia. When I said this over the television, the good, American people came through. Phone calls came in so very fast from all over the forty-eight states. The CBS switchboard in Chicago was flooded with calls. Mr. Framer told the audience that the Colgate Palmolive Peet Company—sponsor of the show—would underwrite the amount of money needed for the purchase of nine tickets round trip to Paris and back. When he said that, I did all in my power to hold back the tears in my eyes, knowing all we had gone through to make this trip. We could now accept the Soviet invite. In fact, Mr. Framer even gave each of us $20 for the trip from his own pocket, and bought us all a Coke.

I personally accepted the invite, I suppose, for fully selfish reasons. As you recall, at that time we all were in the midst of a so-called "Cold War" with the Soviet Union. Nobody went there. None of them came here. My wife was against my going on the trip. My parents were against it. My in-laws were against it. But I went anyway. I felt this was a golden opportunity—I went. While I was away, my wife received many derogatory phone calls.

We arrived in Moscow at midnight on May 9. While we were in Russia, the main subject we discussed at meetings with our hosts was peace between both countries—no more wars. We took a tour of Moscow, saw Lenin's and Stalin's tomb, and were hosted at a special reception in our honor at the American Embassy. Some of the fellows went on a tour of a collective farm while Fred Johnston, Claude Moore, and I visited a synagogue. The nine of us also did some shopping in the GUM department store on Red Square, and attended a special banquet in our honor at the Central House of the

Red Army. There, we met the Soviet soldier who had been the first to raise the Red Flag over the Reichstag.

During our stay in Russia, the Soviet vets graciously accepted us, and showed us a great time. All of us reaffirmed our pledge made back on the Elbe in 1945 for peaceful co-existence and *dignity* between our two great nations.

Three years later—in 1958—a group of Soviet vets came to the U.S. for the thirteenth anniversary of the linkup. They visited my home in New York for a heavy lunch. The following year, I joined Joe Polowsky, Charles Forrester, and some other American vets on a return trip to the Soviet Union to celebrate the fourteenth anniversary. This time, we paid our own way.

Sometime near the end of the war, I had taken part in the liberation of a camp in Germany for forced laborers. I don't know exactly where it was, but I was there. I remember being on a detail that had Germans dig up a mass grave and bury *each and every body* in an individual grave. I shall never forget this as long as I live—the stench was nauseating. Being of the Jewish faith, having seen what the Nazis had done not only to *my people,* but also to people of many faiths, I had sworn when I came home from the war that I would *never* return to Germany.

Yet I did in 1985, on the fortieth anniversary reunion at Torgau.

As I sit and write this, I can only say that I thank God that I went and participated in this great event. I saw not only Americans I hadn't seen for thirty-five years, but also some of the Soviet vets I met back in 1955. I don't believe I can fully express and put into words my feelings on returning to Torgau and the Elbe River, to the places I had been in April 1945 where the memorable meeting of the two armies had split Nazi Germany in half and hastened the end of a very costly war for everyone.

Even now, I can't express my feelings on returning forty years later to Germany and being welcomed as a hero by literally thousands of cheering Germans—adults and children. Yes, thank God I went.

MURRY SCHULMAN was born in 1925 in Brooklyn, New York. He was a private serving with the U.S. Sixty-ninth Infantry Division when he linked up with Soviet troops in Torgau in April 1945. After the war, Schulman was in the retail meat business, then became a wholesale liquor distributor. He is now retired.

36. BUCK
KOTZEBUE

Kotzebue and Alexander
Olshansky standing where
they met in 1945.

Statement in Geneva. November 18, 1985.

I had a great deal of skepticism about the appropri-
ateness, the ability, the rightness of people in our
position trying to urge world leaders to do things
which—pretty obviously—they're trying to do. I
doubt if any of them are coming here with the idea of not achieving
the aims which they have stated themselves.

But it has occurred to me that national policy is frequently dictated
by perceived self-interest, or tragically by over-reacting to events
that take place—witness World War I—or by misinterpreting each
other's actions and statements. But then it occurred to me that in 1945
a group of very ordinary people met on the Elbe River. And at that
time—as Bill Robertson just said—the reaction that we had to each
other was one hundred percent positive and one hundred percent
honest in stating, "Let there be no more wars. We don't want to go
through this again, and don't want our children to have to go through
it."

When I met now Maj. Gen. Olshansky—then a sergeant—in March
of this year, we both said that we would hope that we would be the

last veterans, that we would meet someday when we're old men and there'd be nobody to follow us.

And we did actually have what we felt to be a "Spirit of the Elbe"—we did make an oath. One individual that was on the patrol—we just mentioned—Joe Polowsky, who was my German interpreter, took this so much to heart that he devoted the next thirty-five years of his life trying to keep this alive, often with a lot of ridicule, a lot of scorn, accusations that he was a fellow traveler or a Communist or something bad when all that Joe wanted to do was preserve this very real feeling of friendship that had developed at that point.

Our greatest American president said at another time of great travail that what he was saying would be little noted nor long remembered, but he said, "It's up to us the living here to dedicate ourselves to the proposition that these dead who gave the last full measure of devotion shall not have died in vain." Joe gave the last full measure, and he died in 1983 in the service of humanity just as surely as if he'd died on the battlefield.

I realized then that the least I could do was to try to advance that cause of friendship, participate in it to do what small extent it might contribute. Now, he advocated that we keep this Spirit alive, and we're trying to do that today.

Now we have this momentous meeting here in Geneva between President Reagan and General Secretary Gorbachev. And we ask that they consider not only the ICBMs, and the MIRVs, and the throw-weight, and SDI, but also that they consider Joe and Ivan— the little people—and keep in mind that what they're doing is really a stewardship for their welfare and the welfare of their children and those to follow. They will have died in vain unless our leaders can resolve the differences which so tragically divide our two great countries today. Thank you.

(Novosti Press)

Mayor Strähle (left) places bouquet at Polowsky's grave in Torgau.

37. HORST STRÄHLE

"We will do all we can to preserve the Spirit of the Elbe, the Spirit of Torgau."

Anyone who is familiar with more than the train station of a town, but who has not yet stayed there, often associates the name of the town with ideas gathered from other sources. Torgau. Everyone thinks immediately of a certain Prussian king who fought one of his bloodiest battles just outside the city on the hills around Süptitz, of barracks and parade grounds, of moats and fortifications, of those who profited from wars and from the victims.

But we have to ask ourselves, "Is that really the whole story? Isn't there anything endearing about the town? Can't we trace any redeeming trends?" Yes, we will surely find something pleasant, although it be eclipsed by prejudice and often forgotten. We will find a part of the historical evolution of the town, a picture of the economic development and religious trends of the time. We will find an immortal witness, a heritage resulting from the efforts and abilities of the working people.

We can certainly say that Torgau itself has a great history. It was the residence of the Saxon Electors. It was devastated in the Thirty Years War. Frequent attempts to conquer the town resulted in hard-fought battles right up until the Second World War. At the end of that war, the town unexpectedly made the headlines. At about 3:45 P.M. on April 25, 1945, four American soldiers linked up with units of the Fifth Soviet Guard, which had been on the east bank of the Elbe since April 23. Over the next few days, officers of various ranks held further meetings. In memory of this notable meeting and of the victory over fascism, a Soviet military unit erected the Elbe Meeting Memorial in 1945-1946. On the thirtieth anniversary of the liberation in 1975, the Memorial to the Liberation from Fascism was built.

The year 1945 marked a new stage in the history of our town. Under the leadership of the working class, the garrison and bureaucrats' town was turned into a socialist district capital. In 1953, the reconstruction of Torgau was begun; it evolved into the industrial center of a predominantly agricultural district. At the same time, construction of well-planned modern housing for six thousand residents moved the boundaries of the town west and northwest. The Old town grew up, as did a new center comprised of supermarkets, schools, kindergartens, as well as restaurants and service outlets.

We have clear ideas of how things should develop over the next few years in Torgau. By the end of the decade, every family in Torgau will have a reasonably priced apartment whose size will depend on the number of family members. We will be building a new out-patient facility and will be renovating the hospital. We will construct new restaurants and rebuild many of the old streets, over which more than a thousand years of history have passed.

This is perhaps what Joseph Polowsky had dreamed of. As one of the American soldiers who took part in the historic meeting on April 25, 1945, he chose our town as his final resting place. Since that day in 1945, this man had campaigned tirelessly for the ideal of friendship between the American and Soviet peoples. He had devoted his entire life to peace and understanding between nations. Joseph Polowsky is honored today in Torgau.

On the occasion of the fortieth anniversary of the Meeting at the Elbe, war veterans from the United States and Soviet Union met with each other and with the citizens of Torgau. Twenty-five thousand people took part in this rally for peace, for understanding between nations, for preserving the Alliance of Reason. More than two hundred American citizens were guests in our town. They had an opportunity to judge for themselves how the people of Torgau and the GDR are building upon a foundation of peace.

It was with the greatest pleasure that several of us at the time accepted an invitation to go to Chicago to commemorate the forty-first anniversary of the Meeting at the Elbe. I had the honor of personally participating in this meeting, and was able to convey the greetings of our citizens to the American people. Both we and our American hosts formed indelible impressions of our meeting.

As mayor of Torgau, I am writing this knowing that I am conveying to my readers in the United States and Soviet Union the profound wish of Torgau citizens and of all citizens of the GDR that there be peace and understanding between nations. We will do all we can to preserve the Spirit of the Elbe, the Spirit of Torgau, the pledge taken by American and Soviet soldiers against fascism more than forty years ago. We will preserve this Spirit so that war never again emanates from German soil.

Robertson and Silvashko forty years later.

38. BILL ROBERTSON

"And though we are only two, there are hundreds of millions like us."

I first learned that Lt. Silvashko survived the war when I went to Moscow in 1975 to participate in a US-Soviet commemoration of the thirtieth anniversary of the end of World War II. Ten years later, the two of us met again to celebrate the fortieth anniversary. At that time, I saw him in Minsk, Moscow, and Torgau, East Germany. Most recently, we met in 1987 in Washington, D.C., when he came with Alexander Olshansky to join with US Elbe veterans on the occasion of the Reagan-Gorbachev summit conference.

Alexander remains in good health. He is today the headmaster of a secondary school in the small Byelorussian village of Kolki, not far from Minsk. He has a delightful wife, Zina, and three lovely daughters.

Both of us remain friends. Whenever we're together, we reminisce about the war, about our meeting at the Elbe. I learned from him that the reason the soldiers in his platoon were firing so persistently at me that April afternoon was that the Germans had played a trick on them several hours earlier. Some Germans making a last stand had come out waving white flags, then shot down the Russians who had eagerly come out to the river to accept their surrender. And so now I understand why he was so cautious then.

Alexander told me that the first soldier I met on the bridge—Sgt. Nikolai Andreyev—was killed in Prague a week later while in the Czech capital with the Fifty-eighth "Garde" Division.

The commander of the anti-tank gun which fired at me as I waved the flag from the castle tower is still alive. He is a retired general living in Volgograd, the former Stalingrad. I met him when I was in the Soviet Union in 1985.

But it all happened such a long time ago. It all seems a little unreal now. The lives of Alexander Silvashko and Bill Robertson touched each other briefly, long ago at a faraway river in Germany. The two of us have nothing else in common, do we? I didn't even know he survived the war until 1975— thirty years after our linkup. He didn't know any more of me. And so what do we have to share now other than the memory of a distant, important day in history?

But wait! Both of us, living ten thousand miles apart, still have so much in common. After the war, Alexander Silvashko returned to school, went into education, and became a teacher. He is now a school principal. He married and raised a family.

Bill Robertson did similar things. I went to college, medical school, and entered practice. I married and raised a family. Alexander and I really do have much more in common than just our meeting at the Elbe.

Although we live half a world apart in nations with vastly different ideologies, the two of us share that world. We fought a common enemy more than forty years ago to make this world a better place for *all* people.

I have talked with Alexander about this. We *still* want a better world. We want a better peace than we have had since the war. We want our families to live in peace. We want our children to have hope in a brighter future, to work for what they can achieve and be happy doing it. Alexander and I still hope for better understanding between all nations.

Yes, we really do share many things which transcend our meeting at the Elbe of long ago. And though we are only two, there are hundreds of millions like us.

39. ANN STRINGER

"It is possible for people to get along."

It was not so long ago, was it? The Battle of the Bulge. Our flame throwers pummeling the vaunted Juelich Citadel. The unexpected capture of the Remagen Bridge. And that unforgettable afternoon in Torgau when I saw the young Russian soldier—clad in only a cap and pair of undershorts—running down an empty street, spotting Allan Jackson and me, and yelling, *"Bravo, Amerikanski!"*

We thought then that a new world was opening up not only for us, but also for mankind. For millions of people all over Europe, it really was like coming out of slavery. Those of us who were so close to the fighting had experienced our own personal tragedies. I lost my husband Bill when he was killed in action while reporting for Reuters. Some said I took his place "with tears in my eyes." A needless loss, a needless death, like so many needless deaths in that terrible war.

But still I can't forget the buoyant, boundless hopes of the Torgau meeting, the Russians greeting Allan and me by frenetically firing their rifles into the air, their ebullient shouts of "Welcome, *Amerikanski!*" I remember thinking at the time how all that jubilant gunfire was not from the enemy, but from the Russians— our Allies and friends. In some strange way, it even sounded more friendly, as it most truly was.

No, there was no language barrier that day. Everyone was so glad to be alive. All of us demonstrated in Torgau more than forty years ago that it *is* possible for people to get along, possible for human beings of different beliefs to find common ground. It was a day we should all remember—every year—a day the leaders of our country and the Soviet Union should not forget!

40. BARNEY OLDFIELD

"I can hardly describe the sudden warmth
which descended over our huge table."

There I was on a business trip to the Soviet Union. It was the night of December 2, 1986. The place was Ivanovo, a city about six hundred miles north, then east of Moscow. I was having a big dinner with Soviet trade people. Our host was Vladimir Kabaidze, the Georgia-born, extrovertish General Director of the Ivanovo Machine Tools Plant.

During the toasting, Vladimir said he had met his first American at the Elbe! On checking geography, both of us learned we had been about twelve miles apart when the two armies had linked up along the German river. There in Ivanovo, the import of that event of long ago dropped on me in a most unexpected way.

I can hardly describe the sudden warmth which descended over our huge table. It permeated everything. Vladimir delivered a long toast to me—a fellow "old soldier." The toast brought the feeling of yet another "historic occasion" forming around us, that in East-West trade. If we came to an agreement with him, it would carry with it the memory of another "joint venture" like that which had brought about the great Victory of World War II. The Meeting at the Elbe was a fantastic reference point, perhaps forecasting another joint success.

Vladimir said the first American he'd met had given him a dollar bill on which he'd written his name and address. Kabaidze, in turn, had given the American a ruble with his name and address on it. Vladimir said he'd always wondered whatever happened to that "first American," and that he still had the dollar bill, but the inked address had faded. I suggested that he go to the police to see if they had a process which would make the ancient pen-and-ink legible again. He said he'd do it.

In my toast to Vladimir, I told him how deeply touched I was that we had once been so close but missed connections. With the passage of forty-one years, I added, I was glad we'd found each other there in Ivanovo. I said I was sorry he hadn't been with me on July 1, 1945, when I was in the first American column to enter Berlin. Late that day, I'd done something I'd always wanted to do—gone to the Reich Chancellery, into Hitler's office, where so many of those decisions made had affected all our lives.

The only thing left in the office was Hitler's old marble-topped desk. It had been toppled, but was too heavy for looters to carry.

I thought I was alone, but off to one side was a small Soviet soldier, perhaps from Uzbekistan. He was looking at me very apprehensively. We couldn't speak each other's language, but I waved for him to join me as I moved toward that old desk. He came forward.

When he saw me undo my fly, he broke into a big smile and did the same. It was a very contented tableau as the both of us stood there piddling on Hitler's desk!

I told Vladimir it made me doubly sad to reflect that 1) he had not been the one who was there with me to be a part of this Final Act, and 2) that we had been denied our rightful place in history—participants in the first Berlin act of Soviet-American relations in which there had been *absolute agreement* on what was the right and appropriate thing to do!

COL. BARNEY OLDFIELD, USAF (Ret) was a veteran newspaperman, radio speaker, and motion picture press agent before becoming a career officer. Lt. Gen. William H. Simpson recalled "Barney ran the best press camp in the Army—and incidentally for my Ninth Army." After the war, Col. Oldfield became Director of Information Services for the Air Defense Command. He is currently a consultant to Litton Industries.

41. BILL SHANK

A Christmas Story

When Russian met American in April of 1945, stranger seemingly met stranger. Each was curious about the other. But most of all, those of us who were there were jubilant with the "hope which springs eternal in the human breast." A spirit of brotherhood flowed along the Elbe that April. No politicians were there. Just people. No one was really a stranger to anyone else.

The spirit of brotherhood uniting allies at the Elbe was the same as that which one cold night in World War I caused enemies to leave their trenches to celebrate Christmas together—in no man's land. It was the Spirit of the Elbe which often moved men in uniform to see allies and adversaries as fellow human beings.

In the autumn of 1944, when I was advancing eastward through Germany with the 104th Infantry Division, the Army had rightly forbidden fraternization with the enemy. Yet Providence works in mysterious ways. In one suburb, my section of five came across eleven German civilians—women, children, and an old man—huddled against the cold in a calf stall. One of them asked me, the Conqueror, what they were to do.

A lone, two-story house stood next to the calf stall. The house was empty. I went with one of the women through it room by room. I told her that the five of us would take the downstairs. She and the others could have the rest of the house. She asked me in disbelief, "You mean we can have the *whole* upstairs?"

That night, I was poring over a map by flashlight in a blacked-out room. Suddenly, I heard a tap at the door. Quickly covering the map, I opened the door a crack.

The woman was standing alone there in the dark. In one hand, she held two pieces of black bread smeared with cream cheese and endives. In the other was a glass of milk. Yes, she may have done some mean things in her life. But so have I. So did Saint Paul.

The next afternoon, the five of us left in our jeep and an armored car. The old man, the women, even the little kids stood there waving to us as we drove away. Some of them cried.

Our Division Rear CP was in Stolberg. Near the town, I met a girl who was living with her parents and her two babies, the younger of which was sick. The girl's soldier-husband had been killed in the war. It was Thanksgiving. I gave "my family" some turkey, and wangled medicine from our medics for the baby ...

On Christmas Eve, I came across a large department store in Eschweiler which had been shelled. With a large wicker clothes basket in one hand, I prowled through the abandoned store stuffing the basket with toys, clothes, and a pair of lady's shoes. Feeling like the real Santa Claus, I got in my jeep and headed back for the family in Stolberg. With no top or windshield, with headlights off, I sped in the bright moonlight along a black ribbon of road through fields of snow. Avoiding the attention of our Division CP, I drove up behind the family's apartment house, climbed a drainpipe, and knocked the "shave and haircut" rhythm on their second-story window.

They met me with glee and surprise. At the sight of the new shoes, the girl burst with delight, then cried when they turned out to be a size too small. By midnight, "Mama" had brought in an upside-down cake, some candles, decorations, and a bottle of brandy the family had long been saving for a special occasion. The Spirit of Christmas permeated that room as surely as ever it did a Judean cave.

The Spirit which brought "enemies" together that Christmas in Germany was the same one which flowed along the Elbe the following spring when Russian met American. The Spirit did not need an atomic arsenal to promote it. It was a manifestation of the universal brotherhood which knows neither enemies nor strangers, the religion pronounced in the greatest sermon of all time: "Our Father."

I hope someday all of us will no longer speak of Russians, Americans, Germans, or any other nationalities, but will speak only of *people.* When that time comes, the spirit of brotherhood will truly prevail along the banks of the Elbe, Volga, Mississippi, and every other river on this our earth.

Christmas, 1986

(ADN-Zentralbild)

View of the courtyard entrance to Hartenfels Castle.

42. Studs Terkel

"Imagine what a million ordinary people could do, or two million, or even less!"

My contemporaries—those who took part in World War II—often say, "We were in the good war" or "the last good war" because it was against fascism and Hitler. News of the Holocaust had come out. Let's face it: that war debased and made savages of people, even on the side of what we call humanity.

Many people have forgotten, especially Americans—we have no sense of history. Among many of our young there is no past. There is no yesterday. There was no World War II. A few years ago, a poll was taken, and about forty percent of the kids thought we fought the Russians in World War II! It's crazy. We're the richest country in the world in material things, but the poorest in memory.

Then there was Joe Polowsky—who wouldn't forget. I suppose if there's a lesson to be learned from his short life, it is that he was just an ordinary person with an obstinate sense of history, an ordinary man who had an extraordinary moment in his life.

When Joe met the Russians in 1945, it was his glory moment and—he felt—the glory moment for the world. Once he had his mission of peace, his dream, his persistence—he *was* persistent, oh God how I know—he'd keep after you. Imagine what a million ordinary people could do, or two million, or even less!

The one thing we lack is a certain kind of passion. See, that's what Joe had—*passion*. Passion is an emotion that is unfortunately too lacking these days, not just in our society, but in the world itself. I look for a kind of resurgence of that feeling. Here are the two superpowers about to blow each other up, you know, who once shook hands like *that* in the greatest victory in contemporary history. Joe couldn't forget. Not long before his death, he said, "I believe that as long as *somebody, somewhere* remembers the day when these two adversaries were once friends, there is still hope for the future."

Joseph Polowsky with Elbe veterans in Moscow, 1955.

Alexander Gordeyev kneeling at Polowsky's grave in Torgau, 1985.

43. NORMAN CORWIN

"Joe knew the power of amity, a force greater than all the bombs that have ever been dropped."

Joe Polowsky was ahead of his time when he dedicated himself to the proposition that neither he nor anybody else in the world should forget the fellowship of American and Russian troops when they met at the Elbe and, without being briefed, rehearsed, or counseled, spontaneously threw their arms around each other. Even then, Joe knew the power of amity, a force greater than all the bombs that have ever been dropped.

We have had nearly half a century of cold war between the two giants who were allied in the most savage of all hot wars. A measure of the extent to which both peoples are tired of chronic antagonisms, especially now that our respective military have the capacity to destroy all of us a hundred times over, has been the recent and increasing show of friendship on a people-to-people level—the semi-state visits of little Samantha Smith and her Soviet counterpart, Katerina Lycheva; the tumultuous welcome given to Vladimir Horowitz in Moscow; Phil Donahue getting the go-ahead to broadcast his television shows from the USSR; various live TV exchanges between Soviet and American citizens; the rescue by a U.S. naval vessel of Soviet seamen from a sinking ship, and their subsequent invitations to the White House and to a meal at McDonald's. Polowsky would have enjoyed every one of those.

Nothing is more warming and hopeful, on a broad scale, than evidences of past and present good will, of viable good feeling between nations—the gift from citizens of France of the Statue of Liberty; Japan's present of cherry trees to ring the Tidal Basin in Washington, D.C.; Golda Meir standing beside Anwar Sadat before the Knesset, and handing him a present for his grandchild;

shiploads, planeloads of American food and medical supplies to victims of famine, disease, and catastrophe in the many lands over many years; athletes from a hundred nations, arms locked, singing together under an American moon on the opening night of the Olympics.

Is this sentimental? Was Joe Polowsky sentimental when he strove so ardently to perpetuate the memory of the historic friendly meeting on the Elbe? If he was, then we must all be sentimentalists, and a good thing, too. For are we not touched by a picture of a gorilla petting a kitten, and warmed, almost against our will, by a TV commercial in which a kid offers a cold drink to a bruised and weary football player? Don't we enjoy a gesture as small as a smile and a wave of the hand from a motorist to whom we yielded when we didn't have to?

If a soft answer can still turn away wrath as effectively as when it was first endorsed in the Bible, then perhaps we have not become hopelessly and irreversibly cynical, and there is a chance that one day mankind, a relative newcomer to the animal kingdom, will stop snarling and snapping, and wish to all its members a nice day and a nice year and a nice millennium.

The name for it is peace.

NORMAN CORWIN's memorable program "On a Note of Triumph" was broadcast over CBS Radio on the evening of V-E Day, 1945.

44. Associated Press

"Soviet, U.S. Soldiers Who Met at Elbe Remember in Chicago."

Chicago—Soviet generals carried the hammer and sickle north up Michigan Avenue on Friday, while American World War II veterans bore the Stars and Stripes south, and they embraced when they met on a bridge over the Chicago River.

The old soldiers had met before, at another river in another time.

That was April 25, 1945, on the Elbe River in what is now East Germany, when forward patrols of the U.S. 1st Army's 69th Division encountered the vanguard of Marshal Konyev's 1st Ukrainian Army.

The meeting marked an Allied line across Nazi Germany, which surrendered 12 days later to end the war in Europe.

Friday's meeting was dedicated to Pfc. Joseph Polowsky, one of the soldiers at the Elbe who swore an oath of friendship with the Soviet troops.

Polowsky, a Chicago cab driver who died of cancer in 1983, made "The Oath at the Elbe" his obsession and promoting U.S.-Soviet friendship his life's work.

He wanted April 25 to be commemorated worldwide as "Elbe Day," dedicated to world peace.

When visits to Washington and Moscow failed to achieve that goal, Polowsky stood on the Michigan Avenue bridge every April 25 to plead his cause.

He was dying and broke the last time he took his stand, three years ago, and he announced his wish to be buried at Torgau, where the main linkup occurred.

A news account of Polowsky's death led East Germany to grant his last request.

"We're here because of Joe," said Buck Kotzebue, 62, of Colfax,

California, Polowsky's patrol leader and first American to meet the Soviets at the Elbe.

The publicity surrounding Polowsky's burial spurred the first reunion of the Elbe veterans in Torgau, last year, the 40th anniversary of their meeting.

Kotzebue was one of the Americans who attended, reswore the "Oath of the Elbe," and agreed to meet each April 25, alternating nations.

He grinned Friday at the first Soviet he met in 1945, Maj. Gen. Alexander Olshansky.

"Alexander flew to this meeting and the one last year," Kotzebue said. "Back in 1945, though, he'd walked—all the way from Stalingrad."

Other former Soviet officers at the reunion Friday were Colonel-General Ivan Katyshkin; Major General Alexei Gorlinski, an old friend of Polowsky; and Lt. Alexander Sylvashko.

The Soviet delegation earlier visited Cleveland, Detroit, and Lansing and Kalamazoo, Michigan. They were to visit Lawrence, Kansas, Dallas and Washington before returning home.

"General MacArthur used to say 'Old soldiers never die, they just face away,' said LeRoy Wolins of Chicago Veterans for Peace, which helped organize the ceremony. 'Joe Polowsky said, 'Old soldiers do die, but their ideas don't have to fade away.'"

(Manfred Bräunlich)

Alexander Silvashko (left) with Murry Schulman and John Gillman in Torgau, 1985.

45. ALEXANDER SILVASHKO

"We must now be the best possible soldiers in the fight for peace."

I returned to the Ukraine after demobilization in 1945. The house I'd grown up in, my village were both destroyed. The fascists had killed my mother. My wartime comrades asked me to join them in Byelorussia. I took my wife with me. By the way, she was also a teacher. I graduated from the Minsk State Pedagogical Institute named after A.M. Gorky, worked for a long time in Minsk, then finally settled in Klyetsk District.

Why did I choose to teach history and the social sciences? I love my motherland, and want to know as much about her and to pass this knowledge on to younger generations. In my work, I always try to use more examples of what I myself have experienced and witnessed. I want today's young people to be tempered with the courage, high principles, and moral sentiment of the older generation. Whenever anyone talks to me about the last war—whether in a conversation or as part of a school assignment—I try to make everyone understand, to the depths of his soul, what war really is. They know—everything I say comes straight from the heart. For this reason, lessons about the Great Patriotic War have a special place in our school.

Robertson and I had so many pictures taken of us together both on April 25, 1945, and the following day. But, you see, the best known of them all was taken by an American reporter. I never met him again. But this snapshot first appeared in our country in 1955. At that time, American veterans of the Second World War had invited us to meet with them in Washington. But the meeting didn't take place because the State Department wouldn't give us visas. That was the dismal period that's gone down in history as the Cold War. The meeting took place all the same, but in Moscow. Nine Americans came. They'd fought at the Elbe. Their leader was Joseph Polowsky, who brought a large number of snapshots with him. The pictures were distributed in the hall where our meetings were. Everyone tried to recognize each other in the snapshots. Many of those present were interested that Robertson was one of the soldiers in the photo and that Silvashko was the other. I said a few words. After that, everyone knew me. The following day, the snapshot appeared in *"Komsomolskaya pravda"* and in other newspapers.

Robertson didn't come to Moscow in 1955. He came in 1975 to celebrate the thirtieth anniversary of the Victory. That was the first time since the war the two of us had met. Our meeting was at the Soviet War Veterans Committee. Pavel Ivanovich Batov received us. We talked a long time, reminisced, exchanged souvenirs and addresses. Robertson and I are friends still today. We travel to see each other, we correspond. The friendship born of combat is one that can never be forgotten . . .

On April 20, 1987, an American delegation came to Moscow to celebrate the forty-second anniversary of the meeting at the Elbe. Robertson headed the delegation. Joseph Polowsky wasn't there because he'd died. He'd asked to be buried at the place where Soviet and American soldiers had met. And his wish was fulfilled.

William Robertson is a man of good will. He chose what is perhaps the most peaceful, the most humane of professions— medicine. He learned to make the transition from soldier to doctor. I've talked with him a great deal about his specialty. I've told him about mine—I'm a high school principal in Byelorussia, in Kolki. Just think, I've been teaching for more than forty years now. I can tell you about so many of my pupils.

In 1986, I visited the USA with a delegation representing the Soviet War Veterans Committee. We were in six states, ten cities. Ordinary Americans greeted us with outstretched arms. We even met with businessmen. And so we have a completely different picture now, unlike the one taken in April 1945. Robertson, as a defender of peace, does much to preserve it. Speaking on several occasions before audiences in Moscow in 1987, he repeatedly said that nothing should prevent us from living in peace. That's included in a joint declaration in which Soviet and American veterans reaffirmed the oath which they as comrades in arms had taken to devote their lives to improving relations between our peoples so that there would never be another war. Never again.

Yes, we were pretty good soldiers during the war. We must now be the best possible soldiers in the fight for peace.

Soviet and U.S. vets link arms in Torgau, 1985. (*Erdmute Bräunlich*)

46. ALEXANDER GORDEYEV

"All fifteen thousand people in the stands loudly cheered us."

I have very vivid memories of the meeting of Elbe veterans which took place in New York and Washington in 1958, thirteen years after the Meeting at the Elbe. We were warmly welcomed to America at the peak of the "Cold War." I remember Joseph Polowsky visiting me in my hotel. I can't remember his exact words, but they were something like this: "Alexander, my friend, the Elbe River and the spirit of our linkup must remain an eternal symbol of friendship between the American and Soviet people. We must see to it that no one causes discord between our two great nations."

I remember another occasion when we Soviet veterans were invited to attend a baseball game in Griffith Stadium, where the Yankees were playing the Washington Senators. During a pause between innings, the announcer told the spectators over the stadium loudspeaker that a group of Russian veterans was present. All fifteen thousand people in the stands loudly cheered us, showing their appreciation of our visit and of the friendship between Soviet and American veterans.

Today peace is very fragile and the threat of war indeed great. It is the duty of every person, regardless of nationality, race, or political views, to do everything possible to promote peace and protect life on earth. The veterans whose old wounds still ache should have a special role to play in the search for peace. We must keep the oath we took during the historic linkup on the Elbe and prevent another war. After all, we were once comrades in arms fighting a common enemy.

47. SOVIET AND AMERICAN ELBE VETS

We, Soviet and American war veterans assembled here today forty years after the historic linkup of the allied Soviet and American troops on the Elbe River, once again reaffirm our allegiance to the pledge made by our comrades in arms on April 25, 1945, to dedicate our lives to furthering friendship between the peoples of the USSR and USA so that wars never happen again.

The attempt of the Nazis to insure their world domination during World War II cost mankind fifty million lives. Reminding the world of this grim lesson of history today, when world tensions have reached a dangerous level, we once again resolutely come out for securing the first and foremost human right of all nations—to live in peace, for a cessation of the arms race, and the prevention of a war which can destroy human civilization.

True to the Spirit of the Elbe, we firmly believe in the following:

That we honor our dead;

That we renew and reaffirm our friendship;

That the friendship of the Elbe shall be everlasting;

That we work toward a better understanding and reduction of tension between our two nations;

That we strive for a reduction in both conventional and nuclear arms;

That we diligently dedicate ourselves to mutual respect between our two nations and all other nations of the world.

Today there is no alternative but to live in peace!

Therefore we, American and Soviet war veterans, in memory of those who perished on the battlefields of the War, and those who are no more, and on behalf of their descendants, on this day urge all honest people to spare no effort to avert war!

Yes—to friendly meetings and talks to solve all disputable issues! No—to war!

April 25, 1985
Torgau, German Democratic Republic

48. Alexander Olshansky

"We didn't forget."

In the years since the war, I have met with various U.S. veterans of the Meeting at the Elbe, including Joseph Polowsky, Buck Kotzebue, and Bill Robertson. I also collected all the written accounts of the linkup published in the USSR, and quite a few published abroad. Thus, I learned that Buck's German ancestor August Friedrich Ferdinand Kotzebue, a dramatist and prose writer, served in Russia from 1781 to 1795. Otto Yevstafovich Kotzebue (1788-1846) was a well-known Russian navigator, a captain who took part in Krusenstern's voyage around the world from 1803 to 1806. It was from this voyage that Kotzebue Sound off the coast of Alaska got its name. Buck first mentioned this to me in March of 1985 when the two of us met again on the banks of the Elbe, this time to be interviewed for the British TV production *Yanks Meet Reds.*

In April 1986, Soviet war veterans visited the USA to take part in "Elbe Week." I was a member of that delegation. We visited Ohio, Michigan, Illinois, Kansas, Washington, D.C., and saw so many of our old friends—Buck, Bill Robertson, Charlie Forrester, Don Cole, Murry Schulman, Bill Besswick, Peter Sitnik. Those meetings made us realize that today our two nations should once more join in doing all we can to avert a nuclear holocaust. Together, we defeated a mortal enemy of humanity—Nazism. Just as then, we should today act together in securing a happy future for ourselves and for our children.

While in America, we Soviet veterans visited schools and universities, homes for the elderly, hospitals, an automobile factory, a pharmaceutical manufacturing plant, a number of sports centers, the U.S. Capitol, the White House, and many other sites. The City Council of Dallas made us Honorary citizens of the city. Kansas Governor John Carlin made us Honorary Citizens of the

"Wheat State." While in Chicago, we had an interesting interview with Studs Terkel, then spent two days in American homes.

On April 25, 1986, a symbolic meeting of Soviet and American veterans took place on Chicago's Michigan Avenue bridge. The date was Elbe Day—Peace Day. Traffic on that busy thoroughfare was stopped for the first time in Chicago's history. The meeting ended in a rally. The Soviet and American veterans dropped memorial wreaths onto the Chicago River as a tribute to all those men, women,and children who had died in World War II. It was here that Joseph Polowsky had come every April 25 appealing to his countrymen not to forget the oath that Soviet and American soldiers had taken at the Elbe in 1945, not to forget to continue the fight for disarmament and a world free of war.

We didn't forget.

49. VLADIMIR KABAIDZE
AND FRANK PARENT

"He said that it was midnight, and that he must be dreaming."

From L. Gladysheva, "We Met on the Elbe," Sovyetskaya Rossiya, May 9, 1987

Forty-two years later, on the anniversary of the Elbe linkup, Vladimir Kabaidze, Director General of the Ivanovo Machine-Tool Building Association, found the American lieutenant whom he'd embraced at the Elbe. On the day of the linkup, they'd exchanged addresses. Since neither of them had any other memento to give, the young Soviet officer wrote his address on a ruble bill. It actually wasn't his address, but his grandparents' in Ordzhonikidze, the only home he had then. His father, an Army officer, was also at the Front, and his mother had been evacuated. The American lieutenant wrote his name and address on a dollar bill.

In the decades since their meeting, the ink had faded, making the inscription illegible. All that time, the Kabaidze family had kept that memento from 1945 together with snapshots of Vladimir's wartime buddies.

Late last year, a group of experts from Litton Industries, Inc., came to Ivanovo for talks on technological cooperation. Among them was retired colonel Barney Oldfield, who was active in the organization of the U.S. veterans of the Elbe linkup. He and Kabaidze had met in the U.S. some time earlier. The first question they'd asked each other was, "Is there any chance we met at the Elbe?" But apparently they hadn't. Even though both of them had taken part in that historic event, they'd been twelve miles apart. At a farewell dinner party in Ivanovo, Kabaidze recalled his meeting with a young American lieutenant.

"I'll find him if he's still alive," Barney Oldfield promised, moved by that wartime friendship.

Experts deciphered the faded inscription on the bank note and read the name "Frank W. Parent." Some time later, the former lieutenant of the U.S. Thirtieth Infantry Division, now living in Galveston, Texas, received a phone call from Barney Oldfield. Barney told Frank about his visit to the Soviet Union and his meeting with a former Soviet lieutenant—now the director of an industrial enterprise—who still remembered his wartime buddy.

Frank couldn't believe it. He said it was midnight, and that he must be dreaming. "Anything can happen in a dream," he joked to conceal his emotions. He told Barney that he was that lieutenant, all right, and that he was happy to learn that the Soviet officer was alive and that he had done so well for himself. Frank was genuinely moved by the fact that Kabaidze remembered their meeting at the Elbe.

Now seventy-seven, Frank is a retired geophysicist. His first wife is deceased, he said. He'd hardly be able to find the ruble with Vladimir's address on it. And he kept saying that he couldn't believe it all, that he was so happy.

The next day, Barney Oldfield wrote a letter to Ivanovo which Vladimir Kabaidze received the day before Victory Day.

50. YEVGENY YEVTUSHENKO

In a Steelworker's Home.

I love America,
The America who swam the
Maytime Elbe
holding aloft whiskey
with a tired right arm,
paddling with the left;
yes, and Russia swam to
    meet her in
the Maytime Elbe,
holding aloft vodka
with a tired left arm,
paddling with the right,
and vodka and whiskey—
neat!—without translation
understood
each other perfectly,
goddammit,
on the waters where
    victories met!

I love America,
the America who now
sits with me in the prefab
    ranch-house
of a steelworker.
On the worker's arms
blue veins bulge and fork,
like secret tributaries of
    our Elbe.
There are no governments
    between us now.

Our invisible government
has been chosen by us
    wordlessly—
those same tired soldiers,
boys from Irkutsk and
    Kentucky,
who invisibly swim to
    each other
until today on the Maytime
    Elbe.

Murmuring, murmuring,
invisible waves surge
across the plain fraternal table,
and wineglasses of cheap
    Chianti,
cradled by us on these waves,
redden like guiding buoys.
We talk
as if we were swimming
to embrace each other like
    brothers,
BUT
for twenty years they have
polluted the Elbe.
They've dumped so much
sewage in her—
the backwaters of falsehood,
our era's super-cesspools:
Newspapers soaked in poison,
dregs of inflammatory speeches,
the spit of scoundrels

Kleenexes soggy with snot,
and greasy sweat fastidiously
    wiped
from the hypocrite faces of
long-winded orators.
Beneath the surface of our Elbe
    are hiding
moss-covered mines of distrust
and sleek new submarines
pregnant with torpedoes,
offspring of a marriage of fear
and science.

Oh, when
will we understand each other
as vodka and whiskey
—straight—without translation
understood
each other perfectly,
goddammit,
on the waters where victory met
    victory!
Really, do we need a new Hitler
to unite us
again?
A price
like maybe
much too high . . .
Russia and America,
your path
to each other is tortuous,
but I believe,
do believe
that through all the refuse and
    the mossy mines,
we will swim to one another,
we will swim,
we will embrace

as in the Maytime of '45,
and this time,
I dare believe,
for keeps!
True, the Great Ocean, the
    Pacific, is between us.
But we will swim it;
no ocean so great
it cannot become an Elbe!

I love America,
the America who now,
snuggled in her crib, wiggles
    her delicate toes;
her slender feet shine for us,
    the disenchanted,
like candles radiating hope.
What is her name—
Jan?
Or, perhaps, Lara?
Her eyes
are huge
and blue,
two trusting drops

of that same Elbe,
our common Elbe
we must not betray.
Russia and America,
swim closer!

(Translated by John Updike
with Albert C. Todd)

It has been said that the US and USSR can never at any time in the future become friends. Perhaps. But the lilacs bloom every spring in Central Europe, from the Baltic to the Mediterranean, as they did on April 25, 1945 at Torgau. The mystic chords of memory of April 25, 1945, in San Francisco and the Elbe River are not dead. 1983 is important, but what of 1984 and the years beyond? Something mutually satisfactory in some still unforeseen way will have to be worked out—and all the while Joe Polowsky being buried at Torgau on the Elbe River cannot but have a comforting, creative, positive effect upon events. Please help me. Please help in seeing that I am buried at the Elbe River. Thanks. Thanks to all!

Joseph Polowsky
October 3, 1983

Kotzebue and Olshansky lead commemorative walk down Massachusetts Avenue in Lawrence, Kansas, April 25, 1986. (*Lawrence, KS Journal-World*)